T0197319

Proses, Rhymes, and Something Else . . .

Delf Luis Ross

authorHOUSE

AuthorHouse™
1663 Liberty Drive
Bloomington, IN 47403
www.authorhouse.com
Phone: 1 (800) 839-8640

Published by AuthorHouse 10/29/2016

ISBN: 978-1-5246-4714-8 (sc)
ISBN: 978-1-5246-4713-1 (e)

Library of Congress Control Number: 2016917841

Print information available on the last page.

Any people depicted in stock imagery provided by Thinkstock are models,
and such images are being used for illustrative purposes only.
Certain stock imagery © Thinkstock.

This book is printed on acid-free paper.

Because of the dynamic nature of the Internet, any web addresses or links contained in
this book may have changed since publication and may no longer be valid. The views
expressed in this work are solely those of the author and do not necessarily reflect the
views of the publisher, and the publisher hereby disclaims any responsibility for them.

CONTENTS

PREAMBLE

My drowsy phrase at the age of five or six years old, "The day that I know to read and write" beyond between forests and streams where it was very difficult to want something better, the place that not inspired nor promise a flattering future. But today, God has given me to accomplish my purpose to share with the outside world a personal conviction; life is clean and pure, polluting and damaging, it is negligence, irresponsibility and adversity circumstances which does not allow time to exercise wisdom and intelligence. Personal or family experience base, some images show or illustrate sentimental expression, ideological stance, the belief of any kind and the interpretation of each movement in life.

In order to provide a broader sense; This is a message of reflection and motivation in any circumstantial field which can be used or directed several times, as a birthday, mother's day, father's day, dedication to children; among other many special occasions that can be of great importance for the beings dear or beloved. Making life lighter and more pleasant for those who are nearby or which are far. Sharing best and extolling the excellent with a simple legend.

"Minimizing the bad and eulogizing much of the good news."

DEDICATION

My family and friends wherever they go and are, my gratitude to them always present.

Sincerely:

With love and affection

Delf Luis Ross

1. TRAPPED

The moment that I saw your arrive, without thinking, and without realizing it, you trapped me. Your gaze of affection was the laser that has gone through my existence. The sweetness of your lips, the source of love which I have always wanted. The brilliance of your eyes like two big stars struck the fullness of my life. Your walk to my presence, the rotation of the Earth the floor I walk since the day I came to the world. Your beautiful body, the perfect gift that engulfed my joy. Your smile like a half Moon, the gateway to eternity. Your shining image etched in my memory as a canvas of silk. The perfume of your skin, the breathing space to live the fullness and the delights that are not purchased. Your tender hands like two red roses; symbol of perfect love, the white, your incomparable purity. Your feet, the fortress and refuge in my solitude. I have lost the hope of freedom because I am trapped at the bottom of your heart. Angelic voices lulls me into my deep sleep and locked up in your love absent. My final sentence, it is loving you at the bottom of my being.

2. AS OCTOPUS

Centuries have passed and centuries to come. Generation after generation, prevails his unrelenting harshness. Its insatiable anxiety that dominate the weak. The strong are please without the restriction, and at the powerful tolerates without limit. With the wealthy, it sit for eating. With the criminals makes a pact. He has a personality that is suited to all social levels, and penetrates into the deepest of any category of life. His tentacles reaching every corner of the Earth. There is no place where it does not have presence. Subliminally enters the marrow of his followers, accomplices and victims. Convinces with cunning his executioner, to then, not liberate it or release it so easily. Thousands or million years was born, and baptized with dignity, with elegance, and precious gold for the powerful. Slavery; Yes; I am referring to slavery. It was the cause of death with chains, whips, fire and mutilations to the defenseless and the weak. All Governments, hierarchs, Kings, Princes, clerics, big and small towns or countries, around the world fight with great vehemence but have it in hand to make use of it. Also, they are trapped some large one way or another, and that do not like dropping the weight on them. Thanks to the modern man, it has acquired a lot of new names such as; the law, the regulation, the code, the Constitution, the standard which all proclaim as the triumph flag without leaving aside the development, and technological advancement, scientific, academic and Governmental. His presence and his power will exist around the world. In everyday life, it is apparent generosity to all human beings. When, in reality, it is a trap silent that omit any suspicious sound. Just grab a pen, a pencil, a drop of ink and paper where capture firm, fingerprints, seal or the initials of the identity. Found in all parts of life even on those who are on their way. There is no man or woman that is free from it, any society at any social level is respected. It is a minority benefiting, and take advantage of it while the majority of the population, it is a sword that hurts, and kills slowly until people finish with the strength, and the will of the human being. It has an eloquent name for the strong. Of category and suitable for the weak. Converted as epidemic, plague, and virus or even as a microbe, that is hardly detected the damage and prejudice caused to the innocent. He is honored and exalted with fervor in stands of high esteem. Heralded as a triumph and Crown maximum of a tireless struggle with sacrifices of thousands of lives lost. The powerful political and economic, can break the law at will. Accommodate and tailored at will the misfortune to the rest of humanity. There is no hope that can be fought and applied with dignity. The weak and the helpless, will be the slaves on behalf of the name of the law that is yet unchanged, slavery.

3. UNFORGETTABLE NIGHT

One night I dreamed of giving you my love, and one day dwell in your heart. The doors are open for you to pass freely. Before I see you, and before you ask what belongs to you, beforehand it's yours. The windows are open to circulate our breath without stop. The curtains flutter with happiness seeing the eclipse of the moon with the Sun. The night belongs to us, gathering firewood at the fireplace that it might not turn off not fathom. Near you, smoothly to feel the energy of my skin. Silently cover me with your sweet kisses. Two fine-looking cushions featured for you, and two mattresses where to lay your body. A sigh in the deep fire. A single life pulsating in the background of my being. A single love enjoy forever. Make me to walk in the streets of heaven, and greet the stars with my palms. On the Moon I want to sojourn, and to the world never return. Fly Pigeon, flying my Dove, reach up to the third heaven, and make me scream of joy and everlasting happiness.

4. THE IMAGE

You are very beautiful but your heart is empty.
You look beautiful, but your soul is void.
Your body is a sculpture, and there is no one who values you.
You provoke admiration without feeling full.
You have everything perfect but you just look like an object.
You look very high when your destination is on the ground.
Today you can be remembered and forgotten you tomorrow.
The day that you go, some will weep and others rejoice it.
Your smile is of happiness over your face, it is sad.
You proclaim triumph while hidden failures.
You show great love, but empty by inside.
You shine like the Sun, and darkness inside you.
You dazzle as like the moon but you do not have to light.
You are surrounded by the crowd with the abandoned house.
You are a total deception to those who truly love you.

5. MORE THAN THEM

Look up the eyes to sky, and find a bird fly. His world is an infinite space, and his eternal abode is the tree. One day had nest, another day the branches. He learned to fly without help from anyone. Fell many times but never stayed on the ground. It is a star that you like. Looking and walking knowing that he has no feet or hands. The everyday Sun smile even though has no feelings or emotions. The glow of the Moon, it is the continuity of life. Every twenty-eight days, it renews to illuminate those that rest while others work. Your life is like the Sun because there is no one to stop it. You rest as the moon where everything must be quiet and peaceful. The bird lands on earth only when it is necessary. The other three remain in space as owners, and masters of the same. You, why do not you arise in spite of the small falls that you have, if you are on solid ground, and you are owner of your life. Therefore, you do not stay on the ground, get up and be happy with what you have. Look at the Sun that emits strength. The Moon that gives peace. The star that promises hope. The bird that sings and flies every day without thinking about tomorrow. Live like them, enjoy every opportunity you have, because you do not know if tomorrow you will live or die.

6. LARGE CHAIN

Sincere love surrounded me,
Which did not stay with me.
Angelina gently approached,
Inviting me toward the Hill.
On the sidewalk, I found Basilia,
And we went away from the family.
With Virginia, I started to play,
A place unfamiliar to us all.
Hortensia hang around me,
And she follow me without resistance.
In the distance I saw Imelda,
But I almost end up in jail.
Also, I met an Ignacia,
In fact, she was Anastasia.
I arrived at the house of Susana,
Where I was received by her sister.
Silently it approached Juliet,
Pointed at me with a shotgun.
I reached to the Bella Guadalupe,
And hold her with my love, I could not.
Another day, I was surprised of Dominga,
And I confused her with a Gringa.
Eulalia wanted to steal me,
But Amalia rescued me.
Many times Martha, insisted talking to me
I discouraged it with a letter.
Susy unexpectedly interfered,
And took me to a cute swimming pool.
I loved the beautiful Armida,
With whom I wanted to share my life.

As a stroke of luck, Monica appeared,
Escorted with a Philharmonic band.
Happily Leticia waited on me
And it was to do me justice.
I follow walking as I were lost,
When I reacted, as if I was sound asleep.

7. THE OCCULTISM

Talk about the occultism, it is to think about an evil event. It is to believe in a demonic artifact. It is to imagine spirits and evil angels. It is inserted into the depths of darkness and dense darkness. The religion of all kinds is against such a practice the occultism. Although, the word occult, comes from the verb; hide, that there is derived, hide, keep secret and cover what commonly is known, lying or deception. Great servants of God, preach and teach the sinful is, and which leads to such belief. It is true that there are groups that have made it as devotion, adoration, and service to Satan. Behind the religious scandal, the servants, Governments, parents, siblings, children, grandparents, and throughout society as a whole; each is immersed, and linked to the real occult. Not of belief or of ideas, but of everyday practice each person or individual. Watch carefully what they do not say to your father, your mother, your wife, your husband, to your employer or employee. A man declares his love to you and become your girlfriend or lover knowing that you are married. A woman loving you, conquer and convert it into your secret love. It is not only your love, you keep it because you have children with her. Society itself knows who steals, kills, harass and threat, but does not say to the competent authority at least trying to stop, although the world is full of good intentions. He prefers to hide the evil in his house, town, city or country. If at this time, you cannot call your secret to indicate person, it is the same as hidden. Even if you say, you are not supporter or participant of the occultism, while not revealing you, which you consider harmful for you or another person, it will be more serious, if you keep it until the day of your death. It is best that you act now.

8. THE INSPIRATION

I see you pass on the top of the mountains,
I contemplate your incomparable beauty.
When you walk in the Crystal breeze,
I enjoy the wonders of your figure.
The wellspring of joy and happiness,
Through the hills of the universe.
The lights of your eyes, illuminates those who pose beneath your feet.
Eternal is your love and tenderness imparted at the soul.
Fervent is your love at the dying spirit.
Your remoteness, each time is ever closer,
With the encouraging fragrance to live eternity.
Your presence makes flee time, and the deficiencies no longer exist.
Your image, is a guide with no return direction.
Your hair like the waves of the sea that drowns out the heavy routine.
Your voice as the song of the sparrow that brings joy to the needy.
Your energy lift the fallen without hope.
Your arms the refuge, and your hands a consolation.
So, I say you highness, and I give you my reverence with loyalty.
Your puff instills me life, and the sky it dress formal,
When you rise to the stars.
The inspiration that you convey, it is infinite.

9. WHAT WAS NOT

We could come very far, and fly over long distances until arrive the goal. Let's harvest and enjoy the fruit of our efforts. To live aging and even die together. To enjoy the honey of unconditional love but it was not possible to share the beauty of life. I hope you find the ideal person, you are looking for, and you can love without excuse. One must know and retain the opportunity that comes only once in life, because after that, it does not return where it was rejected. In such a way that no regret nor lament you do today, you have left to never come back. Perhaps someday will be what today is not among us. Hereafter we will walk along separate paths. You will not reach me to know how I am, nor do you miss me as much as absence. You are not mindful of passed love that we had. I carry the affection that for a moment you offered. The love that you gave me, shall be my shelter and shade for my happiness. Our destination will be different but we will always be the best and unique friends.

10. AT TIME

Sometimes what most matters to us, it is worn or is going to never come back. We do not take the time and the opportunity to say; I want you, or I love you. Many times it shames us to express, I like you; for fear of being prosecuted and rightly so, because the values of man has been adrift and on the verge of disappearing. Life is so short and so precious that we sometimes ignore how valuable and how wonderful that is. Better we are dedicated to criticize, condemn and give pity to others. We think and believe that we are nothing loved for anyone. But one day, I received this message from someone important who believes, that I am worth being taken into, and that I am special in life. That I am unique like a Pearl. Perfectible for a better life. Appreciated as an invaluable treasure. At see me front a large mirror, I entered in reason why and how tell me the truth. After a deep breath, I putted the feet on the Earth, and as soon as possible, I send messages to people who are important for me, I made them see how great, and beautiful they are. The good, the excellent, specimen they are, and they share without malice intent. I felt that was my chance at life that I have around me. Now, think you about this. Suppose that one morning you do not wake, you do not see anyone beside you or worse yet, you are not here in this world. Your family and your friends, your classmates and other loved ones, they know, how much you like them and love them? Have proven to them with a salute, a hug or a kiss? Of course, the prejudice and bad imaginations are faster than good intentions. Let all know how you feel, although you believe that they do not love you. It is surprising what two words and a smile can do. In case, if God call me with him, I want to know you, I want you, and I love you with all my being. I ask you to live each day to the fullest, and forgive those that are bad and affront you. You do not keep what hurts your soul but retain what benefits your spirit. You do not insist or cling to something that is not for you or that you left your hands escape. Performs what is within your reach because tomorrow is not promised. It is today, gives us a chance to life. Now, it is the time to live the reality. Not let the courage to ruin your happiness. Not let pride make you lose what you have earned with great effort. Not let resentment to complete with your moment of happiness. Not wait or miss another chance to make someone happy or you the same. Always appreciate and care for those who are with you because they are thinking beings. Not to deliver fully to what is devalued, and lost interest because it is not worth the penalty at the end of the day. You are on time to do everything you want in life without to prejudge anyone.

11. THE NEGATIVISM

Be negative, it moves you away of the person most dear or beloved. It makes sick to whom have trusted you by so many complaints and whining. A negative one, it always remember the past, not because it have learned something good but it still dragging his bad history. All the time, it hoped that he please and satisfy his whims. He do not see other options or find another way. He blames others when failures occur. It seeks to impose its will where it should not be. It want to be included in plans and projects. It castle in the love to receive what has not won. It thinks that always makes more than the other person. It cannot act by itself alone. Someone has to be motivating them continuously. The disorder of his life reflects in the house or at work. To escape of negativism, is a better option but more excellent is to go away than to stay beside personal or private life.

12. IN THE HEIGHTS OF HEAVEN

One of the angels of heaven, has been brought to the world to brighten up and revive the smallest. The most poor, humble and solitary man you look and visit. Because with your beauty, tenderness, love and affection, it is the untold wealth that reflects on your face for anyone who contemplates the brilliance of your eyes. As the Moon in your fulminating glow of night shining from the heavenly city. That inspires poets known friends and strangers to express their intimate and hidden feelings. The magnitude of your beauty covers the imperfection of the world. You surely smell fragrant, incomparable in the life for young and old. Your sweetness, simplicity and generosity enriches the existing. Your smile, that motive and the reason to look at the heights of the sky which is your glory and perpetual abode.

13. AT SIMPLE GLANCE

Voice that gives control and character imposed by authority.
Attitude of supremacy and appearance of strength.
Attractive image and bare sensitivity.
View of eagle and performance of turtle.
Face of humility and countenance of pride.
Soft and light words,
Fulminant echo like trumpet of war.

14. THANKFULNESS

Fortress has been for my life, and hope alive for my future. Freedom you gave me to grow, and the formation of my childhood, the independence. As bud autumn my youth that impossible may have been surviving without you. From now on, I see you, and I will see you with honesty, yearning to become as effective as you. Develop, save and share what I learned of your teaching. Always stretch my hands to the needy without expecting anything from them. I led a high way to achieve what, I am now. In gratitude, I have to do the same with you. While you live near me, I have to enjoy the happiness with white rays many have that fear. You are very special for me to exist, and those who are also far, that love you and contemplate, and admire your great experience. Shared life and age delivered to my existence, your struggle and effort not were, not have been in vain because they gave good fruits. The Summit floor which I stay on today, it is for your dedication and commitment, that I thank you with all my being.

15. IN EVERY PLACE

Wherever you are, the stars embrace you with affection.
Wherever you stay, the glow of the Moon covers you of glory.
Wherever you go, a ray of light illuminates your destination.
Where you see the sun sets, the horizon will be your new hope.
Where you find some roses, you're filled with fragrant love.
Where you find the love of your life,
An angel takes you with protective wings.
Where you feel faint, a kiss of love revives you.

16. PERFECT WILL

I do not know how you are, but I was created perfect. Made to minimal changes in me to be. Gifted with thousand skills that anyone cannot add or remove, what I have, and what I am. My personality is unique. I like to be support but not be a burden. I am of fragile sentiment. Of character relentless against evil and flexible with the good. Tolerant who acknowledges his error. Compassionate with those who suffer. I have dreams to be but not ambition. I defend me from the oppression and arrogance. Pride is my worst enemy. Humility my faithful companion and friend. I see the future with optimism and to last observe very carefully. I live the present time without thinking about tomorrow. My feelings and emotions, I dominate following my own rules. I do not admit them to get in my life, neither permit them, nor send me to do what I do not like. Sicken me the considerations and the preferential treatment. My principle is; serve without meaning. My conviction, not to interfere with anyone or anywhere. I planted myself in a love Avenue. I am going in the streets of affection and good love. Of hand, I walk with the intelligence. In the bed of wisdom, I rest without worry. I come in and go out at the door of knowledge. I drive together with the absolute truth. In favor of the innocent and against the guiltiness.

17. ADMIRATION

I admire your humility, courage, chivalry and your kindness. By recognizing and accepting, something that was beyond all reality including me in your life without being part of it. After so many years, became the final hour. As in all events, I imagine, and I think that it was not easy what you did ultimately. Although they had let you to go from a long time ago, I found too late. It may be that you met by chance. I spoke to you out of decorum and earned you a place here in my heart. I wanted to do something for you, but it was not possible. They did not let me speak or even breathe. They better judged me as a devil and, they condemned me as the destroyer of families. I liked to help you, meet your children and be friends with them would be my delight. The tactics were insufficient talking woman to woman. Forgive me for having failed you, and then having the eyes where I should not. Now, who cares, everything is paid in advance. In all honesty, I must admit that you are a great man and a beautiful human being, for that, I love, I adore, and I love you. You are the perfect man for me and many women would like to have you on their side. A full and thorough man. I admit that, I arrived late in your life. I accept that, I was wrong to say that, that kind of man there was not. I never thought to find one like you. But to have you against me and knowing you closely, convinced me. After being part of your being, I realize as served. I keep the best moments what we spent together. I have memories as a unique treasure in my life. Without any fear, I desire that love that you find, you values, respects you, take care of you, you mime; you want much, love you, that you do not just leave, that never fails you and that makes you very happy. You already know the way of love. You know, what love is and to be loved. Never again the world without light that you went out, live as you are, share with your children all you have. And do not leave for tomorrow what you can do now. Provide all whom you love, and always be happy: my love.

18. ALMOST NOTHING

What you are, I like,
No longer frightens me.
I like your cute lips,
Because your last name is Larios.
Charms me with your beautiful eyes,
And they cause me many cravings.
Capture me your precious charms,
That your voice sings beautiful songs.
Your hair to the middle of your back,
Perfect combination of your blouse and skirt.
There is nothing to question,
Because you put me to tremble.
I would like to laugh out loud,
When I see you smile.
Your walk like shadows of cloud,
Think that you just had.
I saw you as the Moon in its entirety,
And these in your full youth.

19. THE ACCOLADE

You are very beautiful and gorgeous to me. I cannot describe you with high and eloquent words, which may exalt you at the top of the universe. I want to be sheltered with your sublime shade, and feel myself in the middle of your paradise. Charms me to slide me gently on your delicate skin and feel the electrifying vibration of your body. Living in the bosom of your being and from there to taste your sweet lips as a fresh watermelon slice. Feel your hair smooth and glossy emanating from the Summit as a spring that runs through the veins of the passion. Look at you in your eyes and tell you, I love you. I like your dazzling image that has endless wonders. Hear your voice resonate to the song of joy as the breeze of the sea in its waves. Hear the sound of happiness as a campaign that announces the refreshing time of your presence. Your eyes, like the Sun which monitors during the day and the Moon that shines at night to protect secrets. How wonderful is to be on your side and enjoy the fruits of your love. Watch your figure and image, inhale your scent of jasmine. I respond to you without limit and without restrictions. I wish to be yours fully until the last breath and happy forever finding you in my way. Because you are my greatest reward with the most precious treasure in this life.

20. UNDER THE MOON

A hidden and silent witness, is the Moon in its walk of the unforgettable moment of he who lives at full. Intrusively from one extreme to another to observe from the heavens what happens on the Earth. The Moon in its Majesty, shines to infuse confidence and security. Watching on its journey the lovers, witnessing on them through the window with a Whispery voice, sons; I enjoy seeing you together, delivered in body, soul and spirit. Make me feel happy to see two lives turned into a single image, perfect and forever. When she leaves, it takes well-kept all the vivid secrets and experiences which are never repeated. So it may take time and the years without number. It ensures back tirelessly to warn all the movements that, from afar announce their arrival. It is a wonder, pleasure and fortune, be under the protection of a star that never will reveal all the facts, events in the life of man.

21. ACADEMIC OLYMPIAD

Between barriers and obstacles you have raced to reach the goal and get the highest recognition. Sometimes you felt faint but you could master the hidden secrets (**A.B.C.D.E.**) that it demanded greater effort. The A= advances forward although slow and slow. B= Bumps barriers every time they occur on your way. C= continue toward the goal without getting tired or faint. D= Dusting behind any imperfection, error or failure. E= exceeds all expectations to receive the maximum crown which has large steps: **A-B-M-D**. The A= associate degree. B= Bachelor's degree. M= master. D= Doctorate which is the highest summit and the last hill where few manage to get although many attempts. Front of them, you will need will, dedication, and total commitment to climb and succeed. In the meantime, not miss the vision or divert you in the way of knowledge, neither right nor left. Trust in the Supreme Being and yourself. It aspires to reach the highest peak and the maximum chasm, where you will get full satisfaction of having accomplished your goal in the academic Olympiad.

22. WITHOUT ANSWER

Searching for God, it is to find the creator.
Ignoring God, it is ignoring yourself.
Loving the world, is to go to death.
Proclaim God, it is accepting his omnipotence.
You have faith in God, it is to strengthen in the impossible.
Look at the Sun, it is to find darkness.
Observe the Moon, it is to think in another life.
Living with optimism, it is to enjoy the moment.
Love at neighbor, it is also love yourself.
Complaining of work, it is to not have hunger.
To want much money, it is living in poverty.
Search for Jesus, it is to find the Savior.
Walk to Jesus, it is to reach eternity.
Living aimlessly, it is dead.
Speak of God, it is of good news.

23. IN SOME PLACE

Happiness can sometimes be in the desert. Sometimes walking on wheels. It is in the midst of the darkness without company and protection. Other times, it is close without being taken into account. Does not touch soil, does not advance or cannot fly because it has no wings. But it never loses its essence, his integrity, his honor, his loyalty and his faithfulness. It is surrounded by flowers. Covered in butterflies and birds. Waiting to be caught. Only a brave man, a daring, a risky, a determined can achieve to have her in his life, and never release it. Nothing more than there is a requirement to meet be suitable and worthy for her. An irrevocable condition should take care of it, protect it, and defend it up with life itself. There is no technique or magic to change her being, you have to accept that as it is. Complacent for who treats her well. Harmless who it leave happy. Friendly when is treated with excellence. Affectionate when it is being operated with reverence. Available for anyone who wants live.

24. THE GIFT

A gift that cannot be purchased not even with all the money in the world. Gift that comes from the top and that should never be rejected. It is life that is priceless. It is joy that does not measure time. Fortress that does not show weaknesses or defects. It is peace that does not judge, no claims or demands. On its face, it only reflects light like a beautiful star in Blue Springs. His face shines with joy and happiness as the Sun at its zenith. It is daydreaming and pushes laugh unintentionally. It makes cry of joy or despair. It is hidden witness who saved untold secrets. Never think in malice or revenge. It takes part of the misfortunes of others. Screams and cries for unknown pains. It saddens and worries about what he has not done. His smile is incomparable. His feel and look is perfect. A faithful copy of life. By representing it must be well treated with wisdom. It deserves to be sheltered with tender arms offering it any protection that is intelligent. Keep it close with care, affection and love. Enjoy it without conditions, it is the maximum satisfaction. Those, who have it now, congratulations and know how to enjoy the wonders that come from them.

25. CLOSE OF THE SKY

You are radiant as kite and shine like the moon. Your fulminating look like the sun while your image shines like gold refined. Diamond among men and radiant among the thousand stars. Your invaluable figure as the same life that you have a single time. Desired and craved as the great Pearl. As big as the mountain that hill unattainable. Decorated with mountain ranges and surrounded with crystal clear springs. Nature enhances your large and sweet charms. The sea breezes come from afar to cover you with glory. The Sun looks between mouthpieces of the rocks to follow your steps. Shadow and light rules at unexpected moments even those who do not deserve it. It is an honor to visit this poor world who can admire and contemplate its beauty. It is a privilege to have come here to take me to the memory of your greatness. Look out as the greatest in this world is treasure. I do not go nor return, only I only stay where I am. From here I admire and contemplate your beauty. I keep in the deepest of my heart. I take your perfume of love because there are no ladder way in your pleasant abode.

26. MY MOTHER

My mother, so beautiful,
Mommy of my precious life.
Do not cry for what already happened,
Maybe he already was married.
My beautiful woman in the universe,
Laugh with my simple verse.
When I see you cry,
I cannot comfort you.
You do not think more of the past,
So do not let me be scared.
My adored and princess,
From us today, it is our day.
The night is coming,
For what we are going to deliver.

27. THE COURT

Here I am, your honor and jury, invisible and visible before you present: take my relevant declarations and judge it Majesty: I declare, that I wandered in the world aimlessly and without direction. I got lost among the pleasures and delights of the flesh. The privileges that you gave me, I not lived so righteously. The fortunes that you delivered to me, I gave them bad administration. The beautiful gifts that you sent me, were neglected and stepped on its own while I was going through my own course. They grew away from my love and affection. While I had, I did not enjoy it or shared it those who were with me. With my peers, I did very little or nothing. The work and the mission that I had, I did not conducted correctly. The great opportunities I let them go. I have no evidence in my favor because are all against me. I cannot return to the past or recover what was lost, because it is already very late and is not within my reach. I cannot claim innocence because sometimes I failed knowingly and sometimes by ignorance. Adversities were larger and stronger than my own will. I was smaller and vanquished by them. I do not accuse or blame anyone because everyone is responsible for their actions and, I am one of them. Do not ask for condemnation or freedom, only his righteous judgment. I have no visible witnesses who can testify in my favor, only the invisible. They promised to be present in situations like this, despite my imperfections and weaknesses. Trust that you are here until the day today: also declare; that the absent, were always with me and at a most critical time. When I was down, I rose with tenderness. In danger, I was released promptly and took me to a shelter with undeserved attention. In solitude, they were my unconditional company and encouraged me to fight for life. So, I express to this Court: If your understanding and mercy reaches to me, I have nothing to give or pay for that. If your pardon comes up to where I am, I will only give my gratitude. Therefore, you handed down the verdict and sentence that will not hold any appeal because your trial is fair and infallible. Here I am.

28. BY YOUR SIDE

Without it, I would not advance or go far. Walk without your guidance and direction, I would be the end of my existence. By your great love and affection, I have stepped on your side from the first breath. You take my hand to liberate me from the evil way. You embrace me and, give me a kiss when I am asleep. During my sleep you prepare everything so I walk the next day, weeks, months and years. Many are my commitments that I do not hear or listen to what you say or talk me. When you get close, I get only beatings, abuse, insults and claims because things go wrong. None of my faults and weaknesses give you importance because your love and tenderness is perfect. I am delivered on my chores to neglect my children, my friends and all those who surround me. Although I am away from your presence, you try and seek me unconditionally. If I am sick, candles take me to seek health. If I am in danger, you get rid of the death. In hurt, you heal my wounds with dedication and finesse. I am in the dense darkness, there you tend your hand and, lights my way as a great torch out of the infinite profound. Now, I know that I am important and valuable for you. That is why I must always walk at your side because without you, I do not exist.

29. THE DISTANCE

You are a flower that starts to embellish and wear life. A pigeon that begins to fly and travel the world. The fragrance what you want to soak and, you want to pose, it is very high and few leaves left. Go to the Moon, which may guide you on dry land because the Sun is very far and occupied elsewhere. If by some mistake you feel wither, approach the source without contamination so you strengthen it. If for some reason you fall, get up more forcefully and without fainting. Get close to the tree that has many leaves so that you cover in time of heat. Watch the clock without questioning its rhythm and sound that seems to have no sense. Do not look around you but walking forward where you will receive with great reverence and with great honors. First looks for gold and then silver. When the gifts arriving in your arms, take care of them and, protect them from any danger. Even if you are in the jungle, mountain or in the desert, lift your face and fly over them. Strive and try to get to the end of the day. You have much to offer as a flower and be able to travel the world like tender Dove. Fly and sing without desired because the distance does not allow us to be together.

30. OH, LOVE

Two big reasons I have for you,
Two lamps are at your disposal.
This stretched the sheet of silk.
A reserved Eden for us and a sweet source,
The cool pool to swim together.
The steam cloud cover the mountains.
The sun sets and, the Moon laughs.
The stars shine and, the angels sing.
Steps are heard without no one walking.
Understandable and wordless voices.
Oh! You are the love of my life,
How wonderful is to have you with me.

31. NOTHING BETTER

Feel the vibration of your body, it is like riding on a plane without wings. Receive the energy of your being, I relive for a new day. Your warmth transported me out of this world. With you, everything is happiness, peace and joy. To be in your arms, I forget that I exist. Your voice, it is cheerful song every time it dawns. Your image is my shadow and fortress that nobody can have. On your arrival and departure, the door is always open to receive you without asking. I am to hold you, to kiss you and to welcome you. The table is already served and, the same glass I want to drink the wine. The Savannah remains intact hoping that we get together to fly among the clouds and lots. Flower wakes up with your breath and the dove flies with the sound of your footsteps. With your presence, the time is very short and, your return becomes eternal. Sources cry and stagnates the water when you are not with them. Drink wine that intoxicates not and crystal clear water so give life to my existence. Happy twins wait to wrap themselves in honor and, in glory because good manners are without you.

32. CRY AND LAUGH

Crying is a way to unburden the soul out of the feeling that no one knows why one spills tears. Sometimes, gushes crying by a tragedy. For a pleasant moment that shows the deep emotions. By the absence of someone special who cannot be close. Not achieving a satisfactory goal. By succeed without having planned or for not being prepared for that. Other times, it happens because simply life is filled with resentment, bitterness, envy and hatred even one is own. Rarely, he cries for pleasure and taste. No one can feel the expression of the eyes, only those who live it, know the cause and origin. Arguably, it is the ultimate expression of being internal when it reaches its limit. It is the form of cheer to the humble spirit against the angelic sound showing the world the happiness, triumph, achievement or any image that prints tenderness which are of great value. It can also be misleading and fictional because it depends on the circumstances, the time and the place in which it occurs. Both crying and laughing, the two are expression of life that can be weakness or strength. Impossible to know what is behind in every one of them, so it becomes as walls hidden light for freedom or darkness for slavery. Large and small people live it. Others try to guess exactly what is happening. The two flying together like a dove, walk as two children to play towards the garden and surrounded by multicolored Rosales. The Roses smell nice but also have thorns that can make you suffer from which there is to be careful. Cry and laugh, it is good but it has your risk for those who see it and hear it. None of them is forbidden, you just have to live it in their fair dimension, place and time. Both manifest reality, beneficial or harmful to yourself or to someone else. Cries or laughs, that the world knows that you are also human fragile feelings with weaknesses and imperfections. Do not be ashamed of your tears because you are and, only you are.

33. SURPRISE

I went in search of a star,
And it turned out that she was not.
I thought it was a beautiful Princess,
So I went to fulfill my promise.
I walked long and narrow roads,
And was received by her good neighbors.
Hunger and thirst, I got to her house,
They offered me to drink at a proportion.
Apple color but mango juice,
I hear tango music.
I ask, is there anyone at home?
She replied, nobody here and nothing happens.
Confident and sure of myself,
A movement as big earthquake.
And it was not trembling or earthquake,
But if a big fuss.
They were men dressed as women,
Celebrating their great happening.
Who was I? A victim,
To be beheaded without dying.

34. SOMEONE IMPORTANT

A day was walking without company. He has absolute freedom to provide everything you want and could do. He was not going in search of someone special but he met a woman, beautiful or ugly, fat or skinny. Soon after, they began to talk and walk together. Many or few times, they went out to eat, walk or play somewhere. That fate, coincidence or chance, I showed up in the middle of his life. I was born, grew up, and then followed me, others as well who had passed first. Probably was very busy in duties, therefore was not present when I opened my eyes to the new world. As soon he knew and could arrive or wanted to see me, took me in his arms, gave me my first kiss, his caress, affection, love and fatherly love. Those were and are my great gifts in life that, I keep in my heart until today. Else, does not interest me or I want to know if little or much gave me dedication, delivery and care that he provided. It was perhaps not being excellent and admirable. It was not perfect and infallible. But I know that, I live and that it does not let me die. Not one to judge, accuse, condemn the bad or that well-acted. I understand that he did the best thing he could and shared what was available. Did not leave me lying in the street or in the trash, disease or hunger. It ensured my life, health and well-being. Did or made up to where it was possible. His efforts, concerns, sorrows and joys, showed in his face. For this reason, today I tell him with all my heart, with all my soul and spirit; thank you for being my dad.

35. THE SECRET

If time pass a bright star, di that you have not heard her steps or you have seen her picture. You have just had a deep sleep. A wonderful vision. A luminous imagination as the Moon in its splendor. Do not try to follow it or wonder where it goes. Do not try to stop it because it is not for you. It simply clears the way and opens wide. Let it pass and meets the Sun is waiting for she at the altar and be anointed of happiness. If at the end of the day the time walking spent together and accompanied do not be surprised. Give your sincere greeting and reverently to wish them good luck. Sing and be glad that your turn will come.

36. YOUTH

Youth! OH, youth! When will you understand that life is gold and diamonds that the elders would like to have, and which already cannot be returned to the age that you have. You take to lose privileges and fortune laugh, enjoy, cry and sing of joy with all your loved ones closer. See the Sun and the Moon which are never together, each one gives work and rest. When they have a meeting, forget that you are. You think that it is the end of the world. Why are you against and fiddling with against their elders who are not together. You are more valuable and you are like the stars that shine with or without the Moon and the Sun. Be wise and noted, that the stars are small but they are bigger than the day and night. You are like them but forget who gives your life. He always protects you and, cares for you from the sky. Try, therefore, look high and not you so afar it because it is close to. Keep your light and not darkness. Walk right and, never change the course of your left.

37. ANOTHER WORLD

How wonderful to be with you and, what privilege is touching your skin. Great fortune is to feel your warmth as steam that rises from the sea without stopping. Be wearing your hair like foam swab that disappears every imperfection. Inhale your natural scent which perfume cannot purchased. You are as a guardian angel as asleep on a blue canvas. See your face like the Moon in its glory in my awakening. Facing you live another world where the Sun and moon do not exist. The stars are turned off and others are in search of new horizons. The fragrances of the flowers are consumed with your living perfume. The ferocity of the waves of the sea takes another tack to leave us alone. The River Song, spring and supply also disappears by your sublime voice. They are not here and will not return. They have left us a paradise where we will live together forever.

38. THE CHIMERA

One day you came and, you left another day. Since you' have been looking for to be with you. I have traveled sea, cities, towns, mountains, valleys and have not seen you show you up anywhere. Between friends and enemies, I ask if they have seen you but they do not give me any reason. You get out as fog carrying the colors of the Rainbow decorating my life. You took also the footprint of the occasion leaving me orphaned. Now, you cannot see or touch, but I know you are out there. If you give me a signal, it would take less to find you. If I had the eyes of the Hawk, search you from where I am. If I had the skill of a lion, I would distinguish between thousand flowers of the field to catch you as fly. I want to follow you looking while alive because my dream and desire, it is to meet you soon. I have learned that, if I find you. I hold you over what you think and tell us. The world and, I have been searching you all the time because we cannot live without you. If in my search, somebody came to ask, who is and how is called; I will answer with all my strength: happiness! Happiness!

39. LOST TIME

I searched you of the day and night to feel close. I tried to find you in the mornings, afternoons, nights and at all hours. In times of cold or heat, I patiently waited for your arrival. Sometimes, the food had no flavor and was the dream of travel. Minutes and hours, I waited at the gate work and your house. I had enough time to give you a big hug and a kiss. The doors of my house were waiting for your appearance. I offered my hand so that you were my company. I gave you my bed so that you rested on my side. Despite your coldness and distance, I follow you everywhere to feel loved. For you, I took a risk everything to show you my sincere love. Everything, I put in danger my children, my work, my friends and my family to share my love. Many opportunities you had so to stay and were the great lady. Everything was in your hands and your service without conditions. Many tablecloths were filled with dust finally aged. You never appear at the set appointment to walk and run together. I thought that I never tired nor would I realize your rejection. That was lost time which it is impossible to recuperate. Anyway, I do not regret having known you but I weep that it has not aroused before. Your affection was close to me but your love on the other side of the river. Now, I undertook a new course and from now on, you will have to do the same. Build a solid bridge that connect to happiness. If no one comes for you, start your walk without tripping you and do not look at the light that shines in the distance. Leave the past where it is and, sees the future with enthusiasm. I will live the present time to deleting our history.

40. IF SO WAS

If your eyes would illuminate me, could be less stumble in my walk. If your lips belong to me, it would have been where you cool my thirst. If your body was my house, I would not live as a nomad. If your presence was my home, I would not be a generational hermit. If your hair covered me as a waterfall, my dream would be pleasant on my poor bed. If only Y could touch you, my feet would be on solid ground. If your breathing was my breath, I would live with you forever. Ask me where are those who loved me? It left because they do not know love.

Why were they went of my life? Because they did not find what they wanted. That I have affection and love? I have affection and love but who could understand me. That I want you out of interest? No, I do not have interest of through, if it is what worries you. I just want to feel your energy to go on living. I desire at the inhale of the perfume from your body to not pass out. I want to run in veins of your being and, visit all the places where you keep my secrets. Combine what unites us and enlarge the living chemistry. I want to touch your skin soft as silk to feel you close and fortunate. To grow old in your arms and give the last breathe between the sweetness of your lips.

41. DISH FOR BRAIN

Reading silently, is the health of the memory.
Read aloud is the practice of the language.
Thinking, is the fire of the brain to discover the unseen.
To know, is the food of knowledge.
Reading makes the imagination to pass in metaphysics.
Understanding opens the way to prevent a tripping hazard.
To study leads to a better life.
The book, a map and, an address to the unknown.
A pen the silent expression.
Wisdom is the enemy of ignorance.
Intelligence the company of knowledge.

42. INVENTOR AND MANUFACTURER

When a man requires or demands more of what's proper than permissible, he begins to manufacture or devise truths that eventually are discovered and becomes a deadly weapon for good feelings. Aware that nobody is an object in life, man, woman, boy or girl. No one deserves more love or affection, tenderness than good treatment, respect than loyalty, justice than honor and recognition. Women, is no less than the man, or the man is more than the women. No one deserves more protection than benefit. All have the same values although the skill and, capacity are exercised in different circumstances and locations. The right, the privilege, the obligation, the opportunity and the freedom are given equally. The false world has undergone and imposed on humanity that the woman is weak knowing that both are made of the same clay with different purposes. Therefore, none of them can or should ask and demand more than it should. The man and woman cannot nor should demand more sentimental rights and privileges. All individuals should be treated equally even in the smallest detail. As well as plants and animals, they have equality of life developing in their specific areas. The man and the woman are complement one to another. No one is indispensable in their respective lives or required to meet requirements and sentimental or emotional conditions. The richness of feelings is not consumption, supply and demand.

43. GREAT WAILING

I regret having lived under the shadow of life and later find the light of love. I am sorry to have put my children in danger of death. Not having care of them in the house and in all appropriate places. I refused to receive pure love, clean affection, perfect tenderness and good affection of the innocent. I lament unable to recover the time and do not have the necessary means. Rejecting the happiness and the love of my life. I having failed to hold you for my eternal happiness and, by the years that I not googled you with persistence. How much I regret not being able to be with you and have discovered late, that you were not the ideal person for my life. What unfortunate and missed the opportunity to be happy and never returning where it went and who let him escape.

44. THE NEVER

Never lose the vision and the objective to reach the goal.

Never bring what you want to receive or obtain.

Leave the surprise be, then you and you alone will receive the gift of your life.

Never say, I cannot because the force is behind the weakness.

Never stop at what they have proposed you to perform.

Never leave something outstanding to repentance you might not accuse.

Never let grief to govern your feelings.

Never let others take the grip of your life.

Never deny your actions no matter how very dark they are.

Never imitate anybody so you do not lose your identity.

Never change the authenticity of your essence.

Never underestimate your ability and your skills.

Never compare yourself with anyone,

Because each person who is made,

As it is, is designed by the Divine Creator.

45. REMOTE

So I live once I came to the world. I grew up and as soon as I could, I ran away from everyone. My friend who could be, left me early without saying goodbye. Who could be with me, always were far being close. Those who were away, sometimes were and tended me hand. It seemed that it was not part of them to watch them go without saying goodbye. Not only of bread were deficiencies but mostly of love and affection. Now, I feel that I am still equal or worse than before. Much passes between the more distant times, I see them. Their actions are increasingly stronger and as rifles to exterminate its words. I progress as if nothing happened. As if I love the way among them. I try to understand them fully, but sometimes my strength felt faint. Something better I look, love them and accept them as they are. Search for harmony, peace and tranquility. Reach out to all and not be away as it has been all my life by them.

46. CARE

If a love arrives in your life, do not let to go. If it is for you, it will stay with you without your plea and tears. Without supplicates of your knees nor humiliates you before him. The love that you deserve, it is one that comes, stays with you, takes you by the hand and goes with you still in mortal danger. It does not impose its will and change what he do not like. He agree as you are with strengths and weaknesses. It does not say, come, do not ask to stay because one day you will go without compassion. Never walk back because you are dragging it and will be a heavy burden. Do not walk along because you are trampling on it and, you will be a hindrance. Walk to its right side, lean on it when it feels faint, as it let you. Offer your left side so that he rests in you and to re-establish itself. Enable it to acquire greater strength with your support. Give place and respects to its qualities. Don't take into account who is with you and, you fail miserably, never blame anyone. Simply recognize that you have had a failed attempt. You agree that you did not do what you should have done before. The correct application of intelligence and wisdom, is the engine of a good decision.

47. THE BREEZE

The fame, a second pleasure.
The prestige, a moment of delight.
The diplomacy, a usurpation of power.
Personality, a fantasy.
The category, a farce.
The power, a hidden weakness.
The children, the passenger pride.
The wealth, a limited power.
The beauty, a rainbow.
The honor, a presumption.
The justice, a hoax.
The freedom, a dream.
The right law, a trap.
The quality, a lie,

48. WONDERFUL TIMES

Since I came to you, the time has been very short in my life. I always see you as from the first day of our gathering. Everything tastes just as from that encounter. I have been fed with the sweetness of your sweet kisses and the delights of your love. Sheltered with your great love to feel in heaven. The sweetness that flows from your lips, so joy unlimited and comforting to be in your arms. The energy in contact with my body revive the veins of my being. Clothe your shadow angel's is my protection. My output into your abode, I am last breath. You are the living source of which I live. You are the light that glows in my path and that motivates me to return soon. You are the water that refreshes and renews my existence. By your countless wealth I always want to be in you. Between you and me, the time does not exist because we are ourselves. Yesterday never happened and tomorrow will not come. The present, running without stopping and we live it with all the intensity of our forces. We have no need for Moon or Sun. Does not need to take care of us. There who go and we are never alone. Under the shadow of love, continue walking until you get where it is expect of us to the other abode.

49. THAT IT DIFFICULT

What could be more important than health, and essential to itself than life is. Already not yet even think of happiness that a moment poses and then vanishes like mist. Desired amenities or material riches that the powerful to the poor are awarded. Crave the prestige and fame which leads to rupture and endless rift between love and affection. Even the honor is trampled underfoot without consideration. The fundamental rights and justice seem to be irreconcilable. The equality does not come even if it proclaims in the world. The domain and the driving on the truth are absent even though talk or speak clearly. Already, it is no longer equality of gender but the social level, the way of life as individuals, as citizens of each region, country or continent. There are slowly disappearing values of the man who at this time, no one respects or is respected. The world is full of unhappiness that many do not value their own life and less of others. By they kill with weapons or without weapons. They hate and despise without reason. They insult and curse you for no reason. They condemn and judged without evidence. They chase tirelessly swashbuckling. They watch and harass without any merit. Make fun of the innocent and rejoice with the guilty parties. They think that they are masters of the world. They believe that no one deserves to live and enjoy the minimum benefits in this short stay. They take over what is shareable without taking into account who is. They strip and despitefully use without apparent damage. They are guides to perdition dragging behind the weak and ignorant. So many things that happen and occur around, how difficult is to live free of suffering and pain. Both effort and sacrifice what complication, it is to get or be happy.

50. YOUR NAME

Between the abundance of life, your name is Pearl, to call you Bella. From the crowd, your last name is a flower that looks colorful field. I know you're beautiful for decorating my existence. Your nickname is precious that I can only say nice. Your nickname is a red rose which is a sign of perfect love. I see you as unreachable star because guides my steps to get to my house. Your bed of white wool makes me rest confidently like baby. Sublime cloud travel with your perfume of jasmine is my honor. Beautiful Dove, you transported me over hills and valleys to have an unforgettable experience. Each day the light shines to return itself. When I am in you, the fragrance of almond covered me with glory. I rest in your womb of cotton which begins the beautiful eternity. The time passing with the flight of old age. My infinite secret is not to reveal your real name because it is my only treasure.

51. A REQUEST

My love, you are the reason for me to be.
My affection, you are my soul life.
With the breath of your breath, I want to live the infinite moments.
Heart of marble, by your shining happiness in my face.
Oh, beloved, come back soon because I have no life without you.
Dear mine, your face lights up my existence.
I am waiting for your arrival.
My spacious dwelling eagerly awaits your presence.
The moon which commits shines only for us.
The honey which is the source of life,
It runs through my veins to sweeten us eternally.
Revive me with your sweet kisses,
Let me fly over cloud and between glittering stars.
Adorn me with your sexy words.
Cover me with your protective shadow.
Lift me beyond the stars with your fervent heat.
Carry me in your aroma of incense,
And we will cross the sea to not return.
Oh, King; my heart poses which is your perpetual abode.

52. HEAVENLY JUDGMENT

A day on the divine throne, I was accused by the crimes of adultery, theft, fornication, abuse, disobedience, infidelity, injustice and all kinds of legal, social, and religious crimes. Before the supreme judge and jury, I see parading witnesses, some in white dresses and some black. Testimony in favor and also against. The liberation of the jury; we declare us incompetent. It was the time of sufficiency of evidence in its maximum expression. His Majesty rises, the Prosecutor has the word. Without thinking and wasting time. The Prosecutor with an arrogant face and shining countenance of triumph; angrily presents his relevant conclusions. Shown here with evidence of witnesses and victims that: in accordance, all those who contravene the law is worthy of death, therefore, Lord judge and members of the jury; I request the accused the death penalty for the crimes committed since he has use of reason to the day. It has no right to bail, no right to a lawyer. Of course, all tests were against me and there was nothing that I could do or I could say. The senior order that the accused stand up. Supporting myself with my hands on the desk and standing on my feet, I observe a total silence and ask his Majesty; Have you something to say in your defense and of all charges of which you are accused? After a deep sigh, I replied, no Lord, I have nothing to say. Immediately at the main front door of the judgment hall, I hear the voice of a man with resonant echo saying; But I have something to say, slowly opens the doors pair in pair. Surprised the witnesses, the jury, and the same judge by the appearance of the man. All are standing in expectation of seeing and listening to the end of the trial. The judge ordered, come up front and, tell us who you are and what is your name. My Lord and members of the jury, these are my identifications. I am the son of man which the prophets spoke of thousands of years ago. I am Jesus who was born in a manger. I am the verb which acquire wisdom. I am the way to eternity. I am life for those not wishing to die in Sin and being innocent. I am the truth so that they are not unfairly convicted. With all of the above, I am the lawyer of the accused and these is my proof. More than two thousand years, I was judged for sedition and for being the son of God. I was sentenced to death, and death on the cross where I shed my blood to pay all the debt of the defendant. Three days I stayed under the earth to also release those who were no longer in this world. But the first day of the week, I was resurrected to make sure and take care of those who come to me. Today, I ask you, what authority have you to condemn someone who does not know? Someone has died to save this friend and then resurrect? My blood shed on the cross, is not sufficient? Know all that; I have all the keys of prisons and death itself. I have all authority in the heaven and on the Earth, by what I request the absolution of all charges. I order the immediate and absolute freedom of my client. At that moment, I knew that He was my lawyer, since long time ago, he was following me and waiting my case to come to him. I looked for it before out of fear of the damning judgment of others. He won my case and grabbed me by the hand to the door of freedom. His recommendations were; be careful of the brothers of the Church. Take care of your blood brothers. Of the great preachers, evangelists, missionaries and men of renown only seeking their own glory. Your accusers were who you helped in their marriage. You gave them moral, spiritual and economic support. Those who went with you to ask for help, advice, suggestions and sometimes you did not sleep for them. They are the same that you are jealous and accuse you for not departing from the path of God and know that your sins are countless. More they do not see the same which are inserted into their bodies and their minds. Engraved in their hearts that no one can erase. Now, that you are free, remains on the right way. At the end of your life, God will give final judgment.

53. I WOULD

I would like to think that this was a dream,
Although the echo of your voice echoes in my ears.
I would like to believe that I am asleep,
The sound of your smile, it is the musical background.
I would imagine that you are a swamp,
But your picture is engraved on my memory.
I would not to perceive the smell of your perfume,
And feel the cold in my abandoned body.
I would like to never remember your figure and charms,
To not miss the two big reasons.
I would like that the hours and the time does not stop,
To feel that I am not in the world.
I would that all this will end in a second,
By the simple fact of not being together.
I would like the fire of love as the breaststroke,
It turns off at the bottom of our hearts.
I would like to let go and let you go,
Then, wake up to the creator and the just judge,
To listen my final judgment.

54. THERE IS NO WAY

I cannot be against the Government because I am the Government. Against the law I do not want to go because I am the same law. Criticize the rules that governed society, goes against my principle. I cannot condemn social discontent because I am the same right that they all seek and trample with their personal interests. Justice I do not see defect but the actors who pretend to be fair. Fight injustice is to try to kill myself. I cannot go against inequality because I am the same equality that many are unaware of. Incapable of acting against the public or private officials because I am the same official. I cannot go against my own life because I am not a suicide.

55. CONFUSION

I do not know what to do, wake up or remain asleep.
I speak with her without knowing it.
I hear her laugh without having seen her mouth.
I feel her hair that covers my eclipsed face of sadness and loneliness.
I touch her skin without having it in opposite.
The fragrance of her body such as the roses in the garden.
Her eyes incite me to not sleep, day nor night.
Her lips dripping sweet and virgin honey.
Her eyes shines with tenderness.
But between us there is a great distance,
That prevents us from arriving to happiness.
An army without number trying to snatch away the love that we have.
Beset by enemies to deprive us of the love we feel.
We both are encourage to follow fighting for our goal.
Also, we get discouraged then tell us, my love.
Of her voice, I hear a song and,
Of her heart her heartbeat, I listen to the melody.
Sprout drops of joy in her eyes.
Tears of happiness runs in her face,
While my face reflects the abandonment of love and loneliness of love.
I see a star, and more than three come together.
Surrounded by a crowd and, I am aware that, I am alone.
It cover me a bedsheet, and a blanket accompanies me.
I choose a way that drives me to Eden.

56. COME

Prince charming, I want to be yours.
My King, my soul coos for you.
Man of my life,
From you, I am moved.
Your Princess wants to be with you,
I not to make you suffer with me.
We miss your sweet kisses,
Because they are very delicious.
Your loved one and, your Princess,
Waiting for you as a Countess.
We are one of and unique beauty,
You can be confident.
I am here, come, come, come.
My beloved and dear Ruben.

57. GRATITUDE

From the time I came into your house, you gave me the welcome and opened the windows to see the light of day. Without delay, you left the doors unlocked so that I could enter without touching. Thank you for receiving me with elegance and pleasure. For letting me walk freely exploring the richness of your life. Thank you for allowing me to explore every corner of your room. By turning on the light that was off for many years. Thank you for letting me see another way better to live with less significance. Treat me like a great King without knowing me. Receive me as Prince yet to deserve the honor. To make me rest between the scent of your love. Thank you for feeding me with your love and tenderness. By the delicacies served in gold plate. Make me sit on the reserved table that was reserved perhaps for another one. By making me walk on the red carpet without being in the art world and let me pose in a cotton silk-covered bed. My cool parched lips and my deep wound in the soul. To deliver you in my arms and in my life. Forever; thank you.

58. MY GENTLEMAN

My gentleman, do not leave me so, that not to see me lost.
Keep me in your hands to feel protected.
Night and day, I want to be with you,
The desire and the passion, that burns within me.
Commiserate vacuum that is in my being,
Because it is ready in every Sunrise.
Let me travel in your shine light,
Give me the fortune of being your lover.
Come to my house, the doors are open,
To lean out the windows of silk are covered.
I have arranged everything to capture our footprints,
Cover us with the complicity of the stars.
Turn on the fireplace to feel your warmth,
Revive me with your energy without losing value.
Drinking us the perfect love.

59. DOVE AND SPARROW

Two beings who can create and build a new world. Beings who can also destroy all life. From the most humble to the most proud, they pass through them. They can mark the direction of happiness large and small, rich and poor people. No human power there that can avoid of being the most sought after as dangerous criminals. They have no feet for walking or wings to fly, but they haul behind hungry, dying and wealthy. They run at the speed of light from the Sun but trapped like rabbits and locked up in jail. Blamed and sentenced to death although they are innocent. They are monitored as the worst of life and defenseless before their accusers. They get to eat and to drink when their executioner wants. They cry and complain in silence. They prefer death when they are used as objects without life, without affection and feeling. They are always willing to serve for better or for worse. They suffer usurpation and distortion of their essence but, their hearts can never change it. They face all kinds of criticism, disqualification, ridicule, abuse, insult, contempt and curse as if they were the authors of the misfortune. Perhaps for this reason, they are always hidden even against their wills. Rarely receive a good deal and worth being loved. Above all, they have two missions to accomplish. Give life without distinction and maintain happiness when it arrives in your hands. If one day you find the Dove or Sparrow, treat them well, they deserve it largely because they create satisfaction and pleasure. It respects their dignity, because they depend on your life and your happiness. Also remember, that for your own safety, they are not their real names.

60. FGL

(Friend, girlfriend and lover)

Once I met closely, you were my best friend. You were always on the lookout for my personal affairs. As I was at work, in school or how I am at home. You also asked me for my children even without knowing them. Whenever we were together to eat, to study, to work, to walk or to talk somewhere, the time was advancing rapidly towards the Sun. Perhaps, they were the reasons and the motives which led me to confess you from the depths of my heart, I like you, and I want you. Seeing you in your Crystal eyes; I asked with all sincerity: do you want to go with me? You did not pronounce one word, you simply approached your sweet cute lips towards me, and gave me a long kiss as a signal of yes. From that moment, you become my girlfriend more beloved in the life. A woman most appreciated in the world. A lady more cherished by all. A beautiful flower was colorless field to decorate my world. Then sprouted the seeds of joy. From the depths of my being, feelings of love jumping for joy. The paths of freedom were opened. The Sun back out to a new day. The Moon waiting for the arrival of the King. At this time, there was no hidden secret because everything was revealed. The life became a single line to reach the chasm, from the height, toured the mountain without an unseen corner. Sleep, hunger, day, night, cold, heat and the distance, there were no more between us. In such a way that you adorned my existence, giving a sense of value which made me lost. You never ask me why I arrived late or why would not I see you more often. You do not demanded time or asked me for money for you to spend. By the fact of being together, the warmth was the only and the most important thing. The tenderness of your body was enough begging from scratch. The heat of your skin to take and acquire a new life energy. Your words never-heard the song. Your voice, never imagined sound. Your caress impregnated my body, it is the hallmark of an everlasting covenant. FGL.

61. IN THE DISTANCE

I see the way at distant,
So that the past does not reach me.
Persecute me as hawthorns and fallen leaves,
Which penetrates as pain in my being.
I observe the view for the appointment,
And die in the desert, I want not.
Because on the other side of the road,
Someone comes with the same purpose as I.
There is no better happiness,
That the love of my solitude.
You do not search me or come to me,
Because I am happy with you or without you.
At the house I want arrive,
Sodden it of infinite affection.
The happiness I want find,
Walk, live and die without pain.
If at the way I do not arrive,
Leave me where I remain and throw me away.

62. FREEDOM

Freedom, universal female name. Maximum of the country, United States of America's motto. Freedom, it is the pride of Mexico and the deep abyss of its inhabitants. Freedom, it is a dream of the whole, starting with Central of America to South America. From there tour the European territories that words would be missing of listing the cities and their people. Without belittling the streets, buildings and large bridges architectural as on the European continent. Their countries, industries, scientific and technological breakthroughs until it reaches to Canada. Freedom, the demands of modern children and young people who are denied on a large scale. The eagerness of adults that constantly eludes them hands. The freedom that was denied as right of all human beings in the sad planet Earth. Free, finally free, the subliminal message of a few people in the world. Freedom, it is the punishment of the poor and the rich ephemeral flag. Liberty, a poor creature for the universe of mankind. I ask, freedom, my love. Where are you? Why not pull me out of poverty? Why am I in jail without having committed a crime? Why have I under ignorance? Freedom, why I cannot be happy with my love and my life? Why you forbid me to stay with my children? Why do I have to cry and suffer for something that I am not guilty? Freedom, how many times have I waited to make peace in the world, justice for the guilty, equal opportunities for all in this life? I do not request from you for more, I want to live only, and live with you free forever with freedom.

63. THE UNKNOWN

I was a not a great preacher or a poet of renown. I was not a good student, less a grand master. Architect or designer, everything I did as well as I could. I did not walk right impossible to straighten others for their mistakes. I did not have wealth or abundance, only poverty and extreme privation. I dreamed of living in the King's Palace more than I need a hut. In big cities, I wanted to live and, I got between hills, mountains and caves. Wisdom I searched and found ignorance. After intelligence, I went and reached the negligence. When I wanted to become a teacher, I became an inept apprentice. I never asked questions, I devoted myself to give answers I worried others that are not my family. Someone is concerned about me? The Almighty. I always arrived early to start late. I worked without knowledge of a medicine doctor. No title in automotive mechanic or electrician. Neither of plumber, Carpenter, bricklayer, sweeper or beggar. But, I survived and, I had great pleasure and satisfaction to work with full dedication and commitment. Life graduated me and not an academic institution. They saw me very high and large when it was the smallest and most insignificant in the world. Many people believed that I was made of steel, when my bowels were flimsy and fragile clay. They thought it I was a perfect and infallible being, still the most weak and imperfect. I was not a being special or admirable. I was and, I am simply someone who expresses his ideas and interprets the feelings of others.

64. FALSE DOOR

My mother was overprotective of me,
My father scorned me.
All they left me to my fate,
And they hated me until death.
I gave my life to whom I did not love,
Never cared about me where I was.
I have lived full of nostalgia,
Nor the magician could free me with his magic.
My mother went to another world,
Leaving me a deep vacuum.
I was surrounded by so much disappointment,
And I could not find any solution.
My house became like a prison,
That prompted me to commit suicide.
I heard as angelic voice saying; stop,
For you, here I am present.
Between crying and tears, I came back to reality.
I reasoned, asked forgiveness, and I went to another city.
Now, I can face the difficulties,
And combating the many adversities.
I understood that God gave me life,
And it should not be given for loss.
I share with all my experience,
To live with more intelligence.

65. I CANNOT

One and again, I try to forget you. I try not to remember that we live together. With all my forces. I try to not think of you. I struggle not to miss you so much, and tell you that I do not lack. I make it a sacrifice to not want you more. Effort, I will not call to you and ask how you are. I look forward to hate you with all my strength. With the soul I despise you without mercy. With the spirit I do not want to perceive your energy. I want to go very far and not find us anywhere. I look forward to convince me, we never met as we had neither. Never remember the wonderful moments that we share a single bed. I put all my effort to leave in the past. I do delete you in my being. I seek to convert day dark nights, when I remember you. By all means incurred and for having, I have tried to keep you into oblivion. I think that you do not exist or that you are only a perfect imagination. An illusion of my misguided sentiment. A fiction in my sad memory, and fantasy in my poor existence. Your cute lips and your charms, I do not want to remember. Sweets become bitter drink. I have searched tirelessly find someone better than you. I do not want to have you at any time, and do not want to be with you. But, I cannot, and I do not know until when I am going to stop loving you.

66. TOTAL RESISTANCE

Little precious lady, my affection refuses to disappear.
Affection princess, my desire insists having you near.
Star of light, my appreciation is overwhelmingly patience.
It knows that you are not the incontinence.
Little pretty, my affection cannot forget you,
Because you're sweetness and virgin honey has to invite.
My Dove, the fervent pleasure does not want to go,
Beautiful mommy, my love for you refuses to die.
My love, makes me miss what you have,
I miss greatly everything that you are.

67. WE ARE NOT ALL

On the road to life, we find ourselves to be the best partners and friends. The confidants in the most intimate, hidden of thought and feeling. We were always together above criticism. Of the gossip who were dying of envy. We cover ourselves of any fulminant onslaught that surrounded us. We formed a team of work and study, a fortress against attacks by hellish of friends and strangers. Back to the first day of our meeting will never happen in the same way. We identify ourselves as the Bella and the beautiful. Between us, a boss, a refuge and strength. We share a table, a plate, our food, our gratitude and misfortune. We embraced as lovers. We laughed and enjoyed everything as bride and groom. We cried as faithful brothers. We fight and discuss as spouses to settle right away. We support unconditionally. We forgive us the minimum or great offenses. Each who lives his world but pending as we are. All were students and teachers. We see ourselves as more than friends. Respect for our values and dignity is of high esteem and, they were never abused. The differences we had, that were insignificant and major our agreements. We take back what many have not. Respect for the companion. The admiration of what we are. The recognition of what we do. The value that we represent in our lives. The feeling that we keep without prejudice. The strength and the confidence that we are inspired. If life would allow us to choose, it would be the same. Most of the time, it is and will be our faithful witness. And in our memory, an unforgettable story.

68. THE CHILDREN

I had many precious children,
From a distance, I saw them beautiful.
I left them to their fate,
And I forgave myself.
They grew up with many limitations,
And I went after the occupations.
I did not want to be their friend,
For this reason they are not with me.
That was very insufficient timeshare,
For them many days lost.
On their faces shone innocence,
While in my countenance pure incongruity.
Many are in the same path,
They ignore and deny true love.
I recommend you to be a good father,
As also a good mother.
Live like them without any resentment,
It delivers love and good feelings.
They expect much from you, but is not money,
Each opportunity that you have, tell him; I love you.
Love them as your own life,
And you do not confuse them with food.
They are not vain or greedy,
Only they are affectionate and loving.
It receives and valuate it what they give you,
Take advantage of the days of life that you endure.

69. WITHOUT EXIT

I want to run to you but a great chasm stands between us. I do not want to cry for your love much more because my tears are dry by your affection. From the window, I look at you, and the Palm trees will be hiding you from my face. Little by little, I see you straying from my poor abandonment and, you go to an unknown direction. I would like to take you by the hand and say to you, let us go in the upright way. To my disgrace, I have no output to go with you and, it is not fair to wait for me, the rest of your life. My cowardice, is the perpetual chain which slowly will be consuming me. The ineptitude will be my faithful executioner for not knowing how to find the exit. The courage, I was left alone on this closure without bars and padlock. The little force which I had, left me helpless impossible to overcome my weakness. The illusion will be my eternal company. My consolation a hidden fantasy that will always be in my bed. I thought that it would come out here to be confident of your love. I believed that I could fight next to you to dream of happiness. I imagined that, I was prepared to be the depository of your confidence. I assumed that I would be worthy of your love. However, it was my mistake to correspond to you know and dream that you complete me. I stay resigned and tied with my fear. I am worn out before the lack of my value. Defeated by not having the will and the guts of occupying the reserved place. Who occupy the chair in your heart, know she value it, the respect, the love and, she take will take care of you with all the delicacy of world.

70. MIRROR

You are so close that, I cannot feel you.
I am in front of you but, I cannot touch you.
I hear you say, my love without talking to me.
I feel the warmth of your body without you being with me.
I smell your perfume of passion without you by my side.
I cherish your beautiful hair in the vacuum of my hands.
I let you go without releasing you.
Your distance makes me feel your delicate skin contact.
You cannot feel my kisses nor respond to my hugs.
You are very far away, but you go wherever I walk.
In my dreams, your expression of love shines like diamond.
I see you in the past to feel you in my present.
In my solitude, the echo of your voice, it is my perfect company.
Your shadow is a guide in my walk.
When I say, I miss you, you respond; do not miss me, love.
The sweetness of your cute lips, no longer exists.
And my martyrdom, is that you go and come occasionally.
But the heat of your absence how much do I need you.

71. SAFE HOUSE

Keep the door closed so that flies or any insect may not enter, and harm you. Closed a window so that bad news do not enter. The other window, leave it open as an emergency exit. Buy and set curtains up so you cannot see things that you do not like nor you care about. Leave the microphones to capture good news and great songs, beech or no beech party. The visitors may not enter the bedroom nor show you the kitchen you have. Allow, yourself to sit in the room which you fully trust. Take care of Crystal vessels and challenges that do not mix with those of less value. Do not give up the main chair though very elegant as it may seem. Take care your light, candle or the lamp so that you do not make a mistake. If you do not understand what I am saying you, I will give you a few clues. You are the house. The door, is your mouth. The windows, are your eyes. Microphones, are your ears. The others, figure out and be smarter for the sake of your life.

72. FROM AFAR

You look at greatness, and you think that they are lovers.
When they go hand in hand, you believe that they are spouses.
The look that they transmitted,
You imagine that they are gay or lesbian.
To listen and laugh out loud, you deduce that they are happy.
They seem and say, my love, convince yourself of that,
They are boyfriend or girlfriend.
Sometimes you wonder, if they will sleep together.
To see that it is not the husband, you get surprised; it is another!
If not it is the wife, you uproar it; my god!
Although to kiss it beech in the cheek,
You say, that it was in the mouth.
You were not present but you affirm it,
That you saw and heard everything.
You look sitting somewhere in place,
And you conclude that they will later be in the bed.
You are slow to understand but soon to talk and report.
You sigh and surprise what others do,
Although it does not harm you nor benefits you.
You want to do the same as them,
But you cannot because you are not at the height.
To that, you need courage and boldness.
If it is preferable; you need to have no shame.
As you discover what is, better take care of your life.
Monitor your actions and movements at that,
You also have a surveillance.
Stand in front of a mirror so that,
You realize how badly you have lived.
Talk and not scream, judge and not condemn.
Leave others in peace and worry about your good life.

73. NOVENARY

The first day, you were conceived by your parents without knowing who you are, man or woman.

The second day, you were born to start your own life, and create your own destiny.

The third day, they celebrated your birth even though, you did not know or what it was and still you kept doing it.

The fourth day, you abandoned your house to go to school and it was the beginning of the separation.

The fifth day, you fell in love head over heels by disposing of all counsel and warning.

The sixth day, you entered at world of freedom which lasted you very short time.

The seventh day, you married to live in hell or paradise and, it is the most difficult thing in your life. It is hell, if you let yourself be manipulated by your spouse, brothers-in-law, mother-in-law, father-in-law, or the same circumstantial needs. It is paradise, if you are full of joy, happiness, love, affection, understanding and a good deal. If you exercise, your initiatives, plans and projects. Here you should keep in mind that, you cannot already do what you want. Your freedom is restricted with all social and civil laws. There will be a fierce struggle between good and evil. You will need to act intelligently to keep calm and authenticity.

The eighth day, nobody wants it because the problems are set on a larger scale. It causes separation and, family distancing where guilty and innocent pay. Therefore prevents, the misunderstandings and prevail the values of marriage under a cover of love and happiness.

The ninth day, there is nothing to do because it is time of death. It does not come to ask if you want to die or not, is not interested in whether you are, young or old. Get ready because it just comes by you and, not there's no one who can prevent it.

74. TOMB DIGGING

The way to soon reach the grave: is to make life impossible for the person that you love and hate. Envy everything even though very insignificant as it may seem. Celebrate every misfortune that is suffer in his life or family. To wish that the things go poorly and hamper his efforts. That the curse follows his life. Preclude their plans or goals that are proposed. Steal what little they got and throw away and trash the fruit of his effort. Start a fierce persecution, disclosing a dark history. Inventing truths against him. Blame him for the misfortune of others. Despise and hate through death. Do the work of witchcraft or curse. Use any platform or pulpit, politician or clergyman as a forum to judge and condemn. Do hate by that his closest loved. Ask he may never receive the God forgiveness. Tell the whole world that his memories and his presence, make you sick. To execute one of these, you have dug your own grave with irreversible guarantee. Where lies the body but your soul, your spirit and the good feelings that God gave you, are slowly dying by the evil you do against someone and there in the world who can liberate you.

75. ZAR AND SAR

I am going away to start over, and at the sad past never to return.
I want to use my skills, then to not fail.
I look forward to begin, have a new life and to progress.
I see the goal to achieve, with who wants to talk with me.
In my poor common people, I tried to hunt,
Now, I am looking to see if I can get married.
I do not have someone who can embrace me, not anyone who wants to kiss.
Road after road without advancing, I will come to rest at home.
If you see someone trace a line, I ask you to let it go.
The border I want to cross, then; I will lay a repose.
The fruits of my work, I have to enjoy,
It will be with me, what I cannot confess.

76. MY SIN

I confess that my sins are countless.
I wanted to educate my children as I figured the right thing.
Educate them with manners and good customs.
I believing that they had to learn since childhood.
Think and act as if they were adults.
Ask them that they act well everywhere.
They were good and better citizens.
Are better prepared academically so that, they have a better life.
Exercise more intelligence and wisdom for their own good.
Carry further moral, social, spiritual and economic quality.
Closer to God the creator, that it will never forget it.
Live and enjoy the fruits of their work.
Know living in need and in abundance.
Poverty and wealth, they are owners themselves.
And without neglecting anyone.
Keep the brothers unit and the family tie.
Let the good feelings rule inside.
Also give me to work with the idea that,
we do not miss anything.
Believe my decisions were correct.
And certain good for one greater benefit.
I have struggled to obtain material.
Not the proximity and the paternal bond.
My actions were in good faith.
My will without fraud nor prejudice.
I always looked for the common good.
All this was my sin as they made me understand.
Many may be in a similar situation and,
I will say that it is not true.
It is lack of knowledge,

How to manage the responsibility,
And commitments in life.
Understand that not everything is working,
As not everything is family.
There is always an order to follow,
God, self, family, work and, then others.
Do not commit the same sins and be you be wiser.

77. SHARED YEARS

The altar front and before the Supreme Court, I have lived with you the fullness of love. I gave everything to make you happy in good times and in bad circumstances. I battled much to keep me faithful next to you. The enemies prompted me doubting your faithfulness and to end with you. They fought for appropriating love that belongs to you. They came as lions and vultures to snatch me the love, I have for you. Have you next to me, it is a greatness honor. The years shared up to this day, it is a great blessing. Now, my white-haired bear witness to the time not spent in vain. My hands have worn and served to feed us and embrace us strongly with tenderness. My feet do not endure more to take a walk. I see flowers sprout and butterflies flying in the garden. Grasses are also losing their color. My voice, one day stops and you cannot sing more songs of love to the ears. My eyes shortens that I want to have you closer. My pleasant reward is to see you smile without the weight of the years. My confidence is to die with you and, my hope is to expire in your arms. My joy is that you have accepted me as I am, and I am assessed as a great human being.

78. A REASON

I found you to love you,
I came with you to have you.
I gave you all my love,
From you, I am made better.
If you take me out of your heart,
My life has no reason.
I will go to the world lost, wanting you,
I will live wherever, loving you.
The time will help me to forget you,
In the distance I will not search for you.
When your heart is already occupied,
Until then, it will be in the past.
You were my ultimate destination,
Which later has arrived Delfino.

79. YES, I

I left from Villa Hermosa,
To reach the butterfly.
I followed the great Star,
Because she was very beautiful.
I walked a spacious path,
To see my precious.
Many times I've received reproach,
By I did not have a good car.
I will not return from where it came,
By a dangerous boar.
I always think of you,
Of you dreaming of me.
I see you smile, all the time,
Because of this I cannot go.
At every Sunrise I love you more,
Because your great love I prefer.
I go by the Aldama Street,
In search of a lady.
I am in the Center,
To see if I can find it.
If I arrive alone in the House,
It is because something happened to me.
I do not want a visit,
It is better if you do not invite me.
Nothing I have, I have eaten in vain,
And my hand is empty.
I will be busy in my bedroom,
In the company of a camera.
Do not ask me as I am,
Because I will not say where I am going.

Halt yourself where there is love,
I ask you please.
Do not expect my arrival,
I will be with my beloved.

80. LIGHT AND LIFE

Two beautiful stars light my way. Two great sources give me life. Front her glory and sublime shining light, it is your face the offering of grace you are to me. Shining among thousands of stars which shine eternally. Your voice as musical Orchestra the song of the river. Nobility and banner, your image as the same divinity present. Torrent of joy, it is your smile that incomparable refulgent of your beauty. Venerated with honors by the very nature. Your tenderness, Eternal and big, as Queen of the human beings and the universe. Ostentatious and vivifying in life, that only a fortunate man can have you.

81. UNIQUE

Tenderness and beauty has been delivered,
That is the reward for my happiness.
Your angelic voice, the song in my deep sleep.
Your smile, the joy in the awakening,
When the Sun, in each dawn looks out.
Your body the living fortune living full of hope.
Your shade as like a flying cloud,
That it covers and protects my poor existence.
Of the two sources the River born,
Where by large and small is survived.
Bathed in your natural fragrance,
It purifies my soul dilapidated for you.
With your breathing, I come back to live the day.
In you it stay, time is like a second.
Your countenance like the resplendent moon.
Of a promising future.
Your eyes like the rays of the Sun,
Guiding my steps to travel together.
Your hands are the fortress,
Where I want to always stay.
There is no one who can match you because you are unique.

82. GROUP OF FRIENDS

I have two groups of friends who are interested in my life with different interests. The first, finds me to induce me to drug addiction without thinking about my health. Alcoholism to forget sorrow. The abandonment of the study for a degree or professional degree. To take others without effort or without permission. To not respect the elderly, and neither the law in the world of the common order, not even the fear to God. Threaten to whom opposes my will. That they have me as a King in the street. Lord and master in the House. Cornering, hide and unaware of the respect, the truthfulness, the honesty, the humility, the education and the good character of the elementary values of man. The second group of friends, it is opposed to the first. He finds me for who I am as a human being. It is not looking if, I am poor or rich. It does not matter if, I am young or old. If I am of low or high society. It advise me that I work, that I study and that, I take care of my health. That I won't let me be wrap in the vice toward perdition. That I never drift apart from God by badly leaving things. To retain the values of man, which are the food of the soul and live the word of God which is the fortress of the spirit. That, I are always full of admirable virtues. That conserve my roots and my origins. That it respects without distinction and, I valued to everyone by equally. I thought very well and, I stayed with the second group of friends. Now, you choose which to follow.

83. STUCK RIVER

It is more powerful than I.
Larger than my will.
Recorded in my memory without being able to delete.
Impregnated in my feelings that causes me fainting.
Riveted as thorn in my emotions causing pain.
Sharp as a two-edged sword, injuring myself.
Very difficult and even impossible to extract in my bowels.
When I open my eyes, I am in the deep sea.
It is so strong that, I mastered to not be able to get out of it.
It affects me and, consume me without compassion.
I would like to run as the river that serves of something.
Forehead the pain and the tragedy, accumulates as sea or prey.
It sometimes gives me envy towards those who do it with much ease.
Also, it bothers me to not be able to do it.
Because all the sluice gates are closed,
And it seems that the key is oxidized.

Time goes by and I am still at the great Lake.
I feel drown and, I am going to sink,
Without that no one can save me.
My weeping is directed toward the interior.
My tears do not know the external way.
While you can cry, do it with all the freedom in the world,
Leave your tears running.

84. I MISS

My people, I am away from you,
The sadness lives within me.
A great loneliness overwhelms my soul,
In my bed, I cannot find calmness.
I am in an unknown country,
And no one has understood me.
Mine Land, let me return,
Let me see, if here I can progress.
My love, I miss your warmth, and your freshness,
I miss being in you and, with you with madness.
Do not forget me, those who saw me being born,
I wish with all my heart to see them again.
I have lived among many races,
They have also known me.
It is good to be with people of different colors,
But my people and my family are better.
I want to hear the song of the birds,
Not the noise of vehicles or aircraft.
You cannot compare a beautiful building,
With the shadow of a tree.
Streams and mountains, cover me like the first time,
So in my life I never reach old age.
Homeland of my joy and happiness,
Soon, I will go in this city.
Wait for me where we say goodbye,
It does not matter that we are cousins.

85. THE OTHER

The first time, it was easy to cross the border because it did not cost me or knew nothing. I ran everywhere both inside and outside the house. I have lived the delights of this world. From pleasures I have covered myself. I did not want to hear, those who spoke of God because to me, it was crazy. The people that spoke to me of the Church, I judged them as fools. The people who loved me, always were speaking to me of a creator. However, they mixed many real gods, my family, my friends, my job, my fame, my reputation, my wealth and follow my own will. Meanwhile, I was poor although I was filled with money without the help of anyone. So many opportunities came into my hands. Many privileges under my feet. I did not raised my sight to the sky. My occupations were larger. I thought that God was not with me to experience each of the misfortunes. In addition, I thought that for God, I did not exist nor to my loved. Many loved me with sincerity, and others hated me with all their heart. Now, I am in front of the other. Conscious that, with her everything will be different. That errors will never come back to live righteously and correctly. The other, it is a single word and a single decision. The other that I speak, it is death that no one can avoid, and you must be prepared to go with it.

86. MOMENT OF CRISIS

Money to buy is vanished,
And there is nowhere to take it out.
Road after road, it looks for work,
And the salary is very low.
When man goes out of home,
It is to blame him, if anything happens to the woman.
But if it is the woman who goes,
There is no man who goes defensive.
If someone is detected an incurable disease,
The man, the woman, or God himself, is guilty.
A city under violence,
Her inhabitant asks clemency.
If the authority is an accomplice of the mafia,
There is no sane citizen, who she trusts.
The governments are engaged in making war,
Forgetting the people on their land.
My Ranch is called Hot Earth,
They now call it global warming.
Currently already not raining as before,
Everything is the fault of the inhabitants.
Water, every time it runs out,
And it will soon be a single drop.
The felling of trees without measure,
It impairs the health of the environment.
If the same food does damage,
Better see you next year.

87. FORCED MARRIAGE

Unlink you in a moment, and observes, your parents, siblings, neighbors, friends, enemies or your own marriage. Look objectively, the man and the woman are not speaking knowing that they are spouses. They fight it or argue in front of someone. They sleep and eat separately. They do not exchange ideas or talk but impose their will. Outside the house, they show a happy home. Each who attends a different church or at different times. To not look bad, they are active members of a congregation and participate in activities. They walk at distance, and putting the children. They breed children out of wedlock. They have well-guarded lovers or seen many. They are not support nor not help. They accused it and blamed it on each other. There refuge in the vices of entertainment such as sports, music, alcohol, drugs, friends or family. They criticize and insult. They look for and find any excuse not to be at home and less at the temple. They have a terrible relationship but are not separated or divorced. They fear religious or social criticism, so are dead or in sentimental and emotional agony. They are firm to stay together and convinced until death separates them. This type of life, you can only be called, forced marriage. Your case may be equal or similar and, you can give it another name or another definition, you are on your right.

88. BETWEEN PRINCESSES

Two Bella princesses with the brilliance in their eyes and their face which glows, it illuminate the walking of the Bella Queen. Her Majesty before a confusing world, inspires an incomparable and pleasurable life who is worthy to possess it in his hands. Their movements infuse hope as the rays of the Sun in the groves, mountains and in all corners of the Earth. From her birth, the light of the life and, in her being deposited the most intimate secrets of the man. It sprout the springs with the sings of the breeze, and sonorous angelical joy the lonely heart. The beloved Queen, it is like the Moon that monitors their princesses around the world with gigantic steps. While they shine as two star closest to Earth. Like two flowers of the field, it awakes waiting the exit of Sun to inspire tenderness. The Queen gives the fragrance, simplicity, joy, happiness in being and, in the heart of the princesses. Thanks to his Highness, the princesses will be loving and venerating the Queen as unique in the universe. It will cover of the royalty and, they will be happy forever.

89. SURVIVAL

I stayed under large bushel,
Where light never knew.
Which took me by the hand,
Lifted me and was not human.
Pursued me by my enemies,
Abandoned me by my friends.
I followed my path with much sacrifice,
On the verge of falling into the precipice.
I saw near the death,
But I was stronger.
Many prevented to go to school,
Converted as great pain of grinding wheel.
I kept walking among diseases,
With very few friendships.
One of my brothers hated me,
Because I did not participate with the people.
Now, I am happy in my house,
Without looking at anyone who comes or goes.

90. THE VOID

All this time that, I have lived without you, and you are without me a lot. Your go and abandon me, let a vacuum without background where I cannot exit. I live with the nostalgia and, your shadow follows me everywhere. Many flowers try to decorate and fill the void but none reach your height. You were my fortress and your people my last companion. The delicacies that you served me, remain vivid. The slice of cake, I savor it until today. I guard you as a great Pearl in the depths of my being. I always carry you as diamond that enlightens my path. I search you as gold so that, I have no shame. Your absence is the largest and heaviest that any being can suffer. In my dreams, I get glimpses of your figure. Your charms, my consolation. Your sweet tenderness, encouraged me to continue living. Listening to your words, I am motivated to climb big mountains. Your countenance guide me, day and night. I ask you to not send late he who occupies the place to whoever left you, life my not darken. I ask you to not send late he who occupies the place you left to that my life not darken

91. THE COST OF THE ERROR

An error is larger than the universe itself. More effective than the power of an army in the world. More agile than the absolute will. It may end up with the political, economic, social, family, sentimental and emotional world. It is imposed on a more powerful Government on Earth. Tomb at most humble and to knock down at more proud before a failed power. It humiliates the poor before the need and condemns the rich front the incalculable wealth. It can remove the life of the guilty or the innocent, children, adults, elderly, crazy and sane. It does not respect category or social class. It is a silent enemy that it interposes at will, at the friendship, at goodwill and a whole village. It is more dangerous than owning weapons, chemical, biological, nuclear or atomic bombs. Fearsome by all that learned and unlearned, wise and ignorant. It is present in the light and in the dark. By that everyone should be careful to not make any mistake or to continue committing many errors, because late or early always paid the bill up until with the same life.

92. THE DESTINY

Look at destiny from afar,
It is to glimpse a future every day.
Renew until you arrive far,
Without to scorn the good advice.
Adore to the beloved Beauty,
Which it is a reached fortress.
Fly over all barrier as in a race.
At distance to find a large shelter,
But not confused with the ugly refuge.
Believing himself to be a great man,
Even if it has no name.
If it is a haughty woman,
You learn to live in her own way.
Arrive where you want to be,
Well, there you must remain.
Don't cry nor regret because it is your destiny,
Said she that calls herself Constantine.

93. IDENTITY

If you look like someone, you will always be finding where you are. Some will be accepting of you, and desire you as you are but others, will despise you with all their strength. Will always be an unconditional love but also will be hating you until death. Where you hide, they will find you there to prosecute you although you have not committed a serious crime. Who you are, and you being happy, they will be fighting against you, so that you break apart, and abandon the path of joy. You will not be remembered as ever being good but for that you will be truly accepted as a great human being. The love that you shared, will be keep deep in the heart. The affection that you shared, will have fruit without measure. Because it is not the external nor the appearance that makes happy but the warmth human without price stored in the soul. Conserve the best of your life, and discard the worst things about your story. Honor and humility always remain. The sensibility prevails in the life for anyone who wants to take it and don't ever miss your original identity.

94. THE BELOVED

My beloved, I fear that you have send me to the North Pole and leave me to freeze forever. Loved mine, I am in distresses that you send me to South Pole to burn me in the ardent love which I feel for you. Dear mine, it makes me afraid, that you will send me far away, from your life and where I have to suffer much by the absence of your sweet love. Appreciated mine, it scares me, that I be denied the warmth of your love, and your sculpted body becomes property of others. Dear mine, it frightens me that, you get to tell me goodbye at any time. My unique beloved, it oppress me if you say to me until never my baby. Appreciated affection, it frighten me if you were not to be in my love nest. Dear and beautiful lady, without you there is no life. My life, we go walking together. Take my hand and lean on my shoulder. Be not dismayed my heart, I am with you. We are the beloved and, the love that we have, we have decided to live until we die together.

95. GRAY CLOUD

Shared years, hard times. Happy times, sometimes sad. In the middle of the storm, a breath. In the dark nights, it is the vampire. In the background pain, impotence. Among the sea of tears, the mercy. Days of joy, a brief happiness, and times go faster. Between assumptions friends, the interests. In front of enemies, the judges. Since birth we have to spend to survive. Also we have to pay up till die. Disease causes concerns, until neglecting all jobs. Life costs everything in this life, nothing is for free to be pleased. There are only two things that are given away, life and Salvation that comes from God. Health, money, work; friends, enemies, family, come and go. Once dead, will never be back again to this Earth. Be happy with who you are and make happy to whom you have.

96. LEAVE-TAKING

With you, I knew how to distinguish between special and ordinary. Between love and affection. That I do not know how to thank you, I have no how to pay it. With all my heart, I only have four words that I can say; thank you very much: because your love and unconditional given. Your crystalline affection and unique personality in the world. Your simplicity pragmatic in life and your smile that shines as the biggest star in space. Your skin as sliding silk covering all my defects as the only loved being in life. By your radiant presence to look beyond what is visible. You are the awakening that has infused for a new life. An infrared light to walk in darkness and dangerous sidewalks. The kisses you gave me what I will keep them well saved where no one will have access. The secret that you revealed to me will be in the bottom of my heart. The heat of your being will always be the reason for not to limp. For the last time I can express that I love you because I don't regret having known you. And to tell you that I love you because I am not sorry I have loved you with my heart. I arrived late in your life and you arrived early in mine. I recognize that you are great and wonder for the fortune of whom finds you that I am not the worthy. The world has been custom-built that I were not your final endpoint. I am driven to start a new way without return. It urges me to look towards the future and enjoy the uncertain coming. If you find w it first, tell it; he is on his way. If I were first, I will say; she is coming.

97. HELLO

Hello, my great love and loved,
I want to bite you as a donut.
Whenever I tell you come my Conchita,
We will drink coffee with a Conchita bread.
Let's be sure the neighbor will not see us,
If we are in the kitchen.
I will eat you like a watermelon,
Just as my aunt told me.
I will be happy with only a slice,
And the rest I no longer tell the story.
Your brothers went to party,
And we will take our nap.
If because of that you will get paunchy,
We will move to live in another area.
Your parents already gave me permission,
They asked me to be submissive to you.
Your sister is with her boyfriend,
Cenobio picked her up early.
The bedroom is ours, as well the bed.

98. LOVE DISEASES

Love, is not infallible neither untouchable. It also becomes weak and sad greatly. It cries and screams out loud without anyone hears its groan. It slacks aimless and no address when it is left. It is fragile and flimsy in its essence. It can become into warmth and in good affection. In respect and helpful to whom comes to it. Its effectiveness takes another way whenever is attacked or stunned by questions without reason. The permanent doubt about its loyalty. The constant checking of its faithfulness. Its goal is in decline by suspicion. Its purpose is declining when is unfounded prosecuted. It loses interest in demands that are beyond the possibilities. The harassment and monitoring of its acts. That it has to give support for all its movements. Just as; whom do you see? Why are you late? Or why did you get out early? Where and who did you go with? And what did or do? How long did you take? Why you did not tell me? Why you did not take me with you? Do you appreciate me or really love me? Do not you longer like me? You have changed a lot. Is there someone else in your life? Where has the great love you felt for me gone? It seems that I am not worth for you anymore. You have never loved me. You just are with me by interest and convenience. Endless questions that get sick the genuine love and get it tired by the time. It slowly goes far away until it loses or is released by someone. It begins to fly as a dove, the sparrow, an eagle or as the same hawk to find its prey or to be a victim of its own destiny. Love does not die only moves from place and stays where is well treated. It's not all-powerful because it is born and lives among humans. Divine love is the only infinite. It is all-powerful it is not related with men. To love to a loved one, it is not the same as to love God. You may offend God today and tomorrow morning you will wake up with the same yesterday is love. So you have a bad behavior before the Divine Being, love is still perfect and infallible. You do not get sick for any reason the love you have, look after it, protect it and feed it correctly to keep it always with you.

99. INNOCENT

I am not a criminal but I have been treated so. Nor even a thief so I have been classified. I am a being who does not know how to love in perfection, but fights to be in the right direction. The little that I have to love, I try not carry it into the sea. Don't ask me more love besides the one I have because then, because of you no longer I will come. Be happy with what I give you, and always follow me where I go. My love for you never ends, it is only that I was far away from you. Not loving you as you wish, would help you to understand me, if you were in my place. To put it in clear, I declare myself with no fault.

100. BACK IN

I walked unlit having a great torch in front of my face. I guide myself with candles and stable lamps under the sunlight. I left the cotton coat to cover me of rotten withered leaves. My food were dry grasses that drilled my guts. On thorns and caltrops, I slept in the hope of being rescued. Ice was my head-board in order not to feel hit and pain. The only and loyal company, was the loneliness when I was on my knees. Darkness was placed between the fire of living and burning flame succeed. Finally I open my eyes and step on Earth. I knock the door and there is a wide diversity of light reflected in the face of those who expect for me. I am awake and alive, I have come to the perfect love is Paradise.

101. EMPTY HANDED

I do not have an exorbitant or expensive gift to which the world is used. I am lack of soft and eloquent words that could sweeten your ears. I only have and I can recognize your beauty inspiring to live as in heaven. Your beauty decorating my existence in the middle of a desolate world. Telling you that you are very pretty among thousand women in the universe. Praising your gorgeous before the being that loves you unconditionally. You always charming and beautiful anywhere you walk. Also because you are a great lady that there is no way to describe you the highest possible. From my poor and humble floor I contemplate and admire you. I value you for all you represent. I keep you with respect that you deserve. I adore you with total devote self. I love you with my heart. I love you with all my forces. Receive my loyalty and honor as freshly cut flowers from the field. I wish you the best now that you are reaching one more year of life. Be happy in all places and all time.

102. TO ME

You are more beautiful than all the stones of the planet.
A great beauty among all women in the world.
You are more beautiful than all the flowers on Earth.
Brighter than the same stars in heaven.
Covetable by men as the great pearl.
Angeles cried for your abandonment.
The Beautiful celestial city became empty at your departure.
You are more valuable that gold which men fight for.
You are the strength where everyone refuge in time of crisis.
More remarkable that the moon in full.
You are sharping glance as sunlight.
Wanted as the same happiness.
You are all a great fortune.

103. FROM ALL THE GREAT

The Holy Scriptures says; the beginning of wisdom, is to fear God and keep his Commandments. The great philosophers of that time and contemporary have declared that the man has the power to build or destroy their own world. The great thinkers of life, have invented what hurts and benefits humans. Scientists are facing the mystery about how to fight terminally illness and avoid death. The great teachers, have left their footprints in their students' memory. The great servants and ambassadors of God, have left examples of their failures and triumphs in front of the divine presence. The major politicians and economists in the world have implemented the rules and regulations for the common good of society. Many great artists, writers, poets, of all kinds of talents and skills in life, have embodied their works to generation after generation. But the greatest of all the great, is Jesus Christ, the Son and First-born of God. The great Savior of the soul, of the spirit and human life. Of spiritual life for whoever wants to receive it. In where without Him, there is nothing it can exist or move. Now, you; to which one of the great belong you and what is your future after this earthly life.

104. AGONY

I am far away to give you a kiss,
I feel like the same Cherry.
Your lips are such as a Cherry,
That I need so much,
As a strawberry gentleness,
Although I see you too high.
I sing and cry of sadness,
Even more that I keep my firmly.
I dream with you to live happy,
Although you are not an Empress.
Hunger has left me,
And thirst has betrayed me.
Don't take too long to come to me,
So that you can rise me again,
Let me live next to you,
So you can remove my pain.
Get your sweet lips close, to refresh mine.

105. KING OR QUEEN

Many people want to be a King and many dream to be a Queen. All of them yearn to live in the Palace of the King and from there to rule in control of their subjects. If you want to be King or Queen, do not expect love but fear or scares that they will have of you. Do not expect affection but obedience of your orders and decrees. Because of this reason, do not want or look to be none of them, because the King and Queen only know how to order and dictate decrees. Because the place where they are and the exercising role, there is a distance that even between them cannot be together and show mutual love. Better you look for to be a Prince to bring to the Princess and to live in the Palace of love. Look for to be a Princess so your Prince will live in Castle of your heart. Do not fill the Palace of your love with bondage, neither the Castle of your heart with guards, serve and take care of your Prince and your Princess. No one will be better servant than yourself. Do not let in strange hands your Prince or your Princess so gratitude, honor and recognition will be for you. I know a good Prince and a good Princess.

106. I WAS

I was very sensual and also very passionate.
I made every effort to keep myself sensitive.
Not to stop being affectionate,
To see that everything is beautiful.
To feel the magnitude of nature,
And to see all your beauty.
I tried back to be the same,
But I was in a large abyss.
When I saw you passing across as mist,
I decided to wait for you in the corner.
To wake up with your kisses,
And to walk with you again.

107. ALWAYS LATER

First I will rest, after that I star working. I really like school, but I do not like to study. Today I don't have time to anyone, tomorrow I will see if I can attend you. Yesterday was very tiring and I did nothing, I will see later if I can do something. Do not tell me what I have to do I will do later all the urgent. If I feel well, I will go to Church or better in another time. It is time to meet the commitment but I prefer to do it in other circumstances. I always do things later and when I realized, all opportunities have already gone. I have understood that the later, never comes or will come.

108. WHERE GOD IS

From where the view begins as far as the sound quits to hear, there God is. From here, to the bottom of the Horizon, God look at all movement even inaudible. Under white which is the cloud as carpet or cotton, there are families and people who are living under the Divine shadow. Nature as a whole, feeds from the divine source. The whole creation exalts his greatness. God walks on foam as in hyssop to protect his creatures. God is in your breath and in the beat of your heart. He Runs through your veins and preserves your existence. Outside of God, there is nothing to move by itself. All is inside his hands.

109. FRIENDSHIP

Friendship is confusing for some people and for some others a clairvoyant. For the others, friendship always has a personal interest. Only true friends understand it exactly when is not superimposed any special feature. Friendship, is not collective but elective. It is not multiple but unique. It is not required but voluntary. It does not cover the defects but makes us see the errors. It does not condemn but helps to amend errors. It does not sentence but absolves to be free of guilt. It is not able to leave the poor. Friendship is larger than any wealth in the world. It is a refuge for the helpless. Strength for the weak. It comes before all to prevent and correct. It is a perfect comforter in time of suffering. A good company in times of loneliness. It is medicine in hours of disease. A vault that keeps secrets and take them until death. It is better to have the transparent friendship rather than the universe's domain. To wake up next to it because the day is shorter and pleasant. Make worth the friendship you have and do not abuse or go beyond its edge.

110. CUBA

One day I went to visit to Cuba,
In my welcome, I drank a Cuba-shot.
I saw many hardwood palms,
And many beautiful Cubans.
Through the window a grandmother puts her head out of,
To see if someone pass by with a candle.
I had my plasma TV,
And they confused me with a ghost.
This country is an Island,
And I became the island's boyfriend.
It is said here there is no freedom,
But I found a beautiful freedom.
Just for curiosity I went into a store,
But a little Cuban took me to her store.
Under a great Palm tree I watched the sea,
Suddenly a blonde says, I am Miramar.
I got amazed by so much beauty,
I became her slave by clumsiness.
I call by my own experience,
Take care of yourselves and walk with intelligence.

111. – MY WAKE UP

When I saw you, I fell in love of you.
Your beauty bended me.
And your beauty my great fortune.
To sing to you like this, it is my desire.
My great desire is to have you here.
Feeling you close, is my comfort.
To see you going by me,
I saw the light of the day.
To live again, it will be because of you.
From your sweet love, it came my life.
I am here and thank you.
I want to feel myself in your heat.
And in your arms to sing cheerful.
In your presence to live happy.
Give me your love beloved mine.
I want to serve you at your home.
To be with you and love you forever.

112. RECONCILIATION

Two actors who met at job without knowing the purpose of fate. By one year later, they became couple and concerned by being together. It seemed to be inseparable, but one day they had a problem which caused breaking up for two weeks without any communication. Let's call it this event; reconciliation.

General Scene

(After a meeting of students and parents, two weeks after happens all. Neither one dare to communicate in order to restore the relationship so at last, the man takes the initiative, both of them with fear about what to say, they take an agreement and met in a public parking, one when is out of work and the other when the class which attended in the evenings is over. The mystery in here is, what the woman did to be in the appointment, if she worked during the morning, studied in the afternoon and the man was working at night. Without her family realized and suspect something abnormal. As usual, she comes first, soon the man and matches his vehicle.

Performing

Woman. (She puts glass down in her car with a look, I love you and a smile from my love.)

Man. (A gesture of at last I see you) Hello. Good evening. (It was about 9:30 pm.)

W. Hello. Good evening, get in. (In the car of women they shake hands. They felt the need to hug each other but they didn't.)

M. Well, you I called you and I came to talk to you. (Looking facing front)

W. Yes, thanks for coming. Because I also want to tell you something.

M. I want to say I am sorry about what happened the last time we saw. I made the mistake to put you at risk. To be honest I wanted to listen about you, I did not know that you were close to job.

W. Yes, you gave me a serious scare. But I also want to apologies, because I neither behave very well with you as you can say.

M. Don't worry about what you told me, which was a natural reaction that you had.

W. The thing is that I spoke and yelled to you too loud, but then I felt very bad and sad because you had done nothing wrong to find me. So long that we have lived. And I also wanted to see you because I need you.

M. At that moment I didn't want to tell you anything.

W. That was good, you did not pay attention to me.

M. I could have admitted the truth, there is too much between us, so nothing happened.

W. But it is that he started looking for you everywhere. If he found what were you going to do? That caused me to be afraid he did something wrong to you.

M. That won't happen again, that is why I wanted to talk.

W. It was good from you to call me, because I did not find how to talk to you. I felt that I had lost you forever without telling you that never mind. (Eyes filled with tears).

M. Everything is over. The important thing is that we are together, we can talk and make things in clear.

W. I am happy that you did not pay attention to all I told you. I am not so, I lost myself control.

M. Do not worry and there is no problem. Now I would like to know if you want and if you are agree we keep dating.

W. (A few seconds in silence) that is fine, but I am not sure how long it will... I will let you know.

Conclusion: By labor or family circumstances, the actors were transferred to different workplaces, the opportunities to meet as an initiative from man or woman, was so little. At the end, once again, the removal of both complicated to be able to see each other and be together. Time, distance and work were involved without consideration. For reasons are not express, they ended their relationship putting each one's family in the first place. Sacrificing their true feelings and emotions. During the time were together she did all, she went under a fitness surgery even against her own family, only supported by her partner, morally and with phrases such as: do not worry about anything, everything will be for your own good, trust in God and everything will drive well. I will be waiting for you after the intervention. (The man was not there that day, not because he declined but because it was not possible.) He did everything he could, he was always looking after her medical treatment and therapy for six months. He did not pay or co-operated with any penny. They were more than siblings, husband and wife, dating, lovers or friends which is very rare to find someone like this in this world. But soon the end would come in order to be in these terms: by woman side with tears in her face, with her shaking voice and feeling agony, takes her hands impossible love's hands, goes smoothly: before going further, because work, the distance and mainly family, we must stop here, keeping in mind the nice moments. Please do not look for me anymore. Back to where you came from or start another way of life. Look for someone who can be with you with no impairment. Do not call me and I won't either to you for not living more what we have shared during these years. Whenever and anywhere we come across here, we don't ignore each other, be and recognize to each other the way that begins in this moment we will be. It hurts me to let you go because you have made me happy during this time. The man with crestfallen and swallowing his moan just agreed the woman's desire and the will of that Lady. The love he felt for her was so deeply and he didn't want to insist in something that he knew was a transient reality.

Reflection: Whenever there is a feeling pure and clean, it has no price or conditions. When reality is accepted and the common good is looking for there is a new way to be followed. If all of us could understand to others and fix problems advisedly, recognizing the own mistakes, there would be less hatred, resentment, and envy, polluting the soul of innocent as well as own self. Perhaps fate played with them or they mocked destination.

113. THE LAST WAY

I smile to life and welcome to death. Two paths with different purposes and each one offers opportunities in accurate moments. The privileges that life grants, I live up to the maximum and although they go against the moral, tradition or the usual. I always Act without prejudice no one because gratitude of life takes a few seconds. I always have the hope to achieve something better. I know there are more are responsibilities and obligations than the apparent benefits. Nevertheless, I smile to life by the wonderful moments which are countless. I have received too much from it that there is not anything and I find nothing to censure. I cannot complain because the minimum failures because wins are more and pleasant. I also welcome death which everyone is afraid of. Without its coming, suffering prevails, pain, concerns, hoaxes, confrontations and among many other unpleasant events. For some ones, death is a tragedy and life is enemy. Just a few see in death as something undesirable, for others, is a victory. Because leaving this world, it is the most beautiful thing that it can happen. Trough it staying in this life ends and it is the last way to get to the presence of God where we will be judged according to his will. It is good to the ones that we are alive but it is better for those who have been gone. We will continue fighting to survive in this last stage of life while they are sleeping and rest of all in the hope to get to the heavenly throne.

114. CARDINALS

At the North of the planet, the star of joy shines. From the South the fragrance of the beautiful flower gets up. On East is born the light of hope. In the West, the freshness of the living spirit is. In the Center of the Earth, happiness and life are. It is the perfect place where milk and honey flow as spring. Sources sweeten and revive the dry lips. Mountains rejoice when the brave ones climb on them. Waterfalls and springs emit angelic music. The voices' echo, is like the song of the down of day. As beautiful as the same nature, it cannot live without its presence. If something was missing or one of them, it would be the end of the world. There is no place where to go or where to run away because all of them are important and essential in life.

115. HOLY FAMILY

The family that I defend so much and everyone attacks. My family that everyone respect and admire. You ask me, who is your family? I do not know who is or who are. What is my family look like? I don't even know myself, less I know about them. Where is this or where are they? Since I am conscious, I do not know where they are, if they are alive or dead. Have I looked for them? I don't want to know anything that is why it is hard to me to remember and talk about them. Possibly one day they were with me but as soon as crossed the door, they were no longer. Because before I got the world, they left without saying where they were going or when they were returning. I do not think or wish to look for them in order not to face the deadly disappointment. Besides that, they do not know if I exist and live. The time has changed everything for them as well for me. I don't remember when the last time I saw them was. I prefer to continue with my loneliness which does not question where I am going or why I get late. It does not required or claims what I do or stop doing. Distance is my complicit in my deep cold feelings. Disapproval is my strength to show the world what I am worth of. Hate, the reason for living to love who loves me. Condemnation, my absolute freedom when it finds me guilty. The abhorrence, my reason to want who accepts and deserve my affection. Grudge, allows me to acquire energy to face and combat to all. Abandonment is my hope at the end of the day because all my friends gave me by dead. My enemies felt compassion and sorry for me. I am walking without depending on anyone. I have only a faithful partner. A good friend tends a hand to me. His advice is; live to serve and serve to live. Works to live, also live to work. Do not reject to be loved when is properly. I look forward leaving the past where my memory is dark. Now, if you have your family and they are with you, enjoy their presence because soon they will go far from you. If you know where they are, go on you way to live with them. Do not take too long because one day or soon no longer you will have it. It is true you were tried badly or you were damaged. Look for with passion those who truly appreciate your good feelings. If you are welcome, stay there. With trying to do and establishing a relationship, communication and co-existence, you will have got rid from a burden on your soul shoulder. Stay away from the live, living, and from the dead, in death. They are your family but be careful. If they keep in threating you in the same way or worse, don't waste your time and get back to yours. They may not are your blood or have your last name but if they see you the way you are; give thanks to the Almighty.

116. THE REUNION

It passed thousand days to realize how much we loved each other. On hundreds of months the grilled burning of love to our hearts never turned off. From our faces sprang sources of tears covering our existence. Dreams went out day and night since we didn't hear anything from one to the other. We were covered with cry and sorrow due not to be able to be together. At some point we felt like being in a dead end street and the world came over us. The richness of feelings that we reserve and keep no one could take it off. Spaced between kilometers and thousands of hours we survived the darkness of love and tenderness. Now last chance has come in our hands to finish what that day started. It's time to recover what we left pending on the way. It is time to live the fulfillment and delight of happiness in our being. Given each other in soul and body, it is and will be the maximum crown of our life. When love were consummated, we can shout it to the whole world we have reached the hill and we are happy. The dark past is no longer exist because our love is pure and perfect. The time and the distance have gone in order to join our lives. Overall, let's keep love as volcanic fire without stopping. And let's always be happy for all the days that are left.

117. ONE LOVE

My great love is the nature,
And I also love Teresa.
I love so much the beautiful Leticia,
While I still think of Alice.
I miss Margarita a lot,
That was waiting me in a border.
I would like to forget the beautiful Brenda,
But I keep her as a garment.
The more the days pass slowly,
I miss the beautiful times of my youth.
From time to time Hermelinda visits me,
But she always meets Rosalinda.
I am annoyed to be alone,
I realized that I am in Abasolo.
A little town that is in Guanajuato, Mexico,
Still far from the Pacific Ocean.
Whenever you want to see me in my Palace,
You have to get it slowly.
In my time I was called the humming-bird,
Supposed because I used to walk from flower to flower with a Rose.
Actually I am not someone important.
But I wanted to be a great singer.

118. A DAY AS TODAY.

It has been wonderful that you've come to this world. From thousands of angels you went out and you traveled among a thousand of stars. From the crowd of flowers you fell to be worshiped with loyalty and honor. Everybody knees in front to your presence and image such as the same divinity on Earth. It is impressive to see you smiling and to hear your resonant voice as a trumpet to attend at your calling to service. Choirs and celestial chants tagged the steps in your walk. White Carpet is the cloud in which you walk around gently. The nature tries to set in your throne in which you are, where the light of life is born that flows without stopping but it will never reach your height. I wish to serve you with all my heart and worship you with all my love as you deserve it. I really want to wake up in your arms each morning and tell you, I love you. May the night does not get late to keep be sleeping in your pleasant breast and to tell you, I love you. In all times and places where you go, I will keep you always humbly, truthfully, with respect, faithfully, with justice and with all the honesty of my existence. Because one day as today, you got into my life. You fell in my arms and I you let me enter inside you to be part of you. Only one day as today.

119. I WAS GONE

I had to leave the house because I got tired of waiting for you. I even left the city in order not to meet you. And I did not want to answer the phone not to hear your contempt words. I did not read your posts any more as a mourning signal of your love. The letters expressing love became into a sweet hate. I got falling in love with you deeply just like you did with me. There were several years of fight and effort that hardly will be deleted. I realized that getting away each other was the best that I could do to not to hurt us more. You may be very happy with her and you also with him.

120. IT IS NOT FOR MONEY

It is important to listen to others, indispensable to listen to others.
It is necessary to lift the fallen, compulsory to fill in the command.
It is recommended to follow the rules and preventive measures.
To look at others' defects, to correct our own.
Do not underestimate the poor and humble, neither enlarge the rich and wealthy.
To work to get satisfaction, not because an exorbitant salary.
Living quiet and peaceful, for a happy ending.

121. CHANGE OF DIRECTION

You performed on my way it was not an accident. I walked along with you it was not by chance. You gave me your hands not because compassion. I made me participant in your life not because you felt sorrow. You let me rest in your heart without having the right. Your love was the exit door for a new life. Your love the awakening from the bottom of darkness. Your personality and character to live again. Here is where has started the walking to new horizons. Everything seems to be unknown and confusing. I wonder, where must I have arrived? I find and see many ways. Many wide open doors, and some other locked with the keys placed on them. A situation which I have to live and choose accurately. It is very difficult to passing this firing test. There are also two stones on the way, preventing get into one of them. Stands a large desert and a bottomless abyss. I am facing a big Mountain and behind an uncertain future. But your angelic voice's echo, there so far and in my walk, I hear to say, with or without me, you have to move on. I confess that without you it has been very complicated, and it has been too hard to take you out from my heart. With you it could have been easy to rebuild my life. It also could be very different to perfect what one day we joined. But to get back where we started, it is impossible. It's only left to look the clock advances in its normal rate. To walk is what I can do throwing down barriers. To feel the time which every day is shorter. I must go on and get the first to everyone. It is my chance to take advantage of opportunities to come. To fight without pass out until the last time. To get the final goal which is my hope to rest up forever.

122. THE EFECT

The stars shine of joy because your walk among them. The sea waves rejoice with your brightly presence due this they make a rainbow where you can go through with honor and glory. The Oceania follows your steps which a shining mirror of gratitude. Flowers flutter thankfully with your sweet breath. The river plays the passionate melody to pose happily. All look at you as if you were otherworldly. You walk silently to not interrupt my sacred dream. My joy is to see you passing in front of me. My happiness is to contemplate you as the goddess of the universe. I can't reach you because your speed is light while I am slow. Only your fullness inspires me to keep living and feeling as the only loved in your presence. You're always with me and you are my true company. I am happy because you are my special and maximum gift.

123. WITHOUT ANYONE

Nobody is essential to achieve the proposed objectives. No one is important to reach the goal. With the own effort and willing all is possible in this life. With totally self-giving and dedication, it is enough to reach the crown. And it is not a fact of pride where you've come but a blessing that will bring you long-term satisfaction. It is necessary that you keep walking forward a clear. Later large honors are waiting for you, acknowledges and congratulations that will be reward your constantly fighting. Think of getting far away no matter what others say, think and make. Appraise your life because you are never or will be alone although you don't see anyone around. There are a few who try to make you fail but many those who are with you to motivate and help you to open the sidewalks in despite the narrow and dangerous they appear. Take advantage of all the opportunities which get in your life and don't look back neither remember the bad history. Ignore what happens around you and advance on any impediment until getting the biggest award you have wished. At the end of the day you will live with the result of your efforts which will give you peace and serenity to your heart.

124. FATAL LANDING

After living together for a long time, we both planned to travel long without untie hands. We decided to take the ship off believing that we were prepared to do so. We ignored all warnings about winds and storms. We dreamed to fly on all odds that were in the air. We wanted to live by the stars and cover us with a cloud as our perfect sheet. To show that we are the best pilots of our life. We joined our powers to pass over all barrier in the flight. We left all to live our genuine love. All was going well until the third part of the flight, when the enemy with their lethal weapons reached us to avoid our purpose. Despite our long resistance, we were surrounded and attacked with anger. We lost strengths and control that we did not have time. We fell as a bird without feathers or wingless chicks. We were wounded and hurt for weeks or months and our soul became healed. My co-pilot lost all interest to keep fighting. Today we sometimes see each other and we do as possible not find us. We fight to understand why selfishness is bigger than goodness. We are no longer together neither we will because we are afraid to have the same or even more pain that we experienced. We do not like resignation but it is the only resource that remains.

125. THE INCOMPETENCE

You are not useful for a good husband as I am not able to be a good wife. Both of us have failed on to not know how to manage and cope with the love that sets us in one way to go. We hurt each other unintentionally, we hit us without any reason with words, gestures, looks and attitude. It is in a risk our children's happiness as well of having our good example. It is too much better to be as friends and to live as good siblings. A difficult stage to overcome in which time is the only master that will make us to learn the lesson we had. We will have to share what we could not as husband and wife, to do what we didn't as siblings. To strengthen us as excellent friends, admirable peers and best neighbors. Society will be in charge to judge us, the children will have doubts. It was not fate which made us to fail but unwillingness to build a good destination. The world will condemn us as unsuccessful while God will have the last word.

126. WALKING

I walked in the middle of desert and among mountains without finding water or people who could help me. There were many days and lost years between drought and spiny herbs. Sometimes sleepless or without eating to get to the river that infuses breath of life. I neglect myself as well to others that were still helpless. I tried to get where someone or no one had gone before to refresh my dry lips with the heat in summer. In the chilly and freeze winter I crave to cover myself of tenderness. I looked for living under a sweet life source but I sheltered under dead trees. I know that in the other side of the Mountain is the spring, the source which is forming a grounds to mitigate my dryness. Those who are on their way, keep going and don't stop. No one is going to come for you and I will be waiting for you there because stopping on the way I must have finished.

127. THE JOURNEY

Traveling through times and spaces, is a great fortune. Moving on multiple roads, is to live in total freedom which others have no. The sidewalks are marked with traces in order not to fall in the same empty. Surfing large gaps, paths and tracks looking for a better future. Major towns, ranches, fields, Estates, colonies and cities welcomed me. Many houses, huts, caves, tunnels, buildings, castles, mansions and strengths, where I were received in welcome. At the same time, rivers, lakes, beaches and seas opposed to me to not continue my course. Strong torrents and blowing winds, tried to divert my endpoint. Hurricanes and tornadoes came to destroy my achievements. Sea waves wrapped me to drive me drowned. Many misleading lights overflew spaces to not find to you. Darkness and shades surrounded me to put end to hope. Huge challenges appeared that seemed as an infinite to get where you were. I have seen me in good opportunities, but they could not stop me. Bad times motivated me to continue harder. At the middle of the trip, a great battle to choose between thousand options. I went tempted to leave the way, but the fire and the desire to progress, were engines to get where I'm now.

128. AT THE MID OF CENTURY

Fifty years of failure and triumph. A non-return course the unattainable distance. At the mid of century, a dominated summit by too much effort and sacrifice. The many expectations, have been fulfilled but others quite on the way. I have been witness of many pleasant moments as well as bitter times. I have lived and seen around. Shearer events and non-renewable stages. I have served well for a few and bad for others. The past, is a mirror where to see defects and correct them later. To see the virtues for strengthened and keep in the best attributes. The future, is a dream that is full of kindness and wonders at the end do not exist. The present time is the beginning of the end in where everything will become the same as in the first steps of my existence. A present time that I must have to live fully while the Sun goes and shines every morning.

129. SMALL RECIPE

It is very easy to react drastically to an unpredictable situation or even knowing what will happen. The Sun turns off. The moon is hidden. The stars fall as sand of the sea. The doors and all roads are closed. The world is converted into darkness and there isn't anyone to whom trust. Everything seems that the end of the world or life has come and is unavoidable. But actually is not like that, because all you can solve with no precipitation. Whenever you discover a lie or deception from your woman, man, daughter and son, is still one of these steps that will help you before you act with determination. Control your emotions without asking why. Control your character to not to increase the problem. Take time enough to think about what happened. Don't hear but listens to what the others tell you. Keep a spirit of humble. Collect all the necessary data that are true and reliable because it can build you in a trap. Look for professional guidance and counseling. Do not go to co-workers or classmates because they will be in your favor even if you lose. If your life isn't in any danger, do not respond to the defensive. Remember that all the things happen by induction or provocation. The one who commits the lack, not precisely is the one who is wrong. You may be the cause. If you feel that your dignity, honor, right, and freedom was damaged or affected; stay away from that person. Ask always for a second opinion with experts. They have no titles or graduated, they are specialists in practice but not in theory. Take the time and the strength to analyze the things with a humble spirit. Asks wisdom and look for God's direction and you will feel better than before.

130. THROWN OUT

The whole world may be against you. Your parents might take you out of their lives with all the right they own. Your siblings can hate you with all their heart. Your friends' contempt as breaststroke flame. Your enemies' curse burning up to death. Those from who you were expecting support and understanding, left, and abandoned you. Once you thought that people in Church were a refuge but were very wrong. Gossip, criticism and many actions against you, were bigger and powerful. The last thing you expected to hear, was this, I do not want to see you again. You have no room in anywhere and walk around aimlessly. You look around and no one is there for you. They do not let you enter into the Church neither in your own home. They consider you as a pestilence and filth of life. Those who you met before, are found on the road but you are a strange. When they speak, you hear voices about you are lost and you are a waste of the world. Because these causes and some other more, you decided to go far away from all of them but there is always one more who stays by you. He can never dispose someone because his love is infinite. In his face there is understanding and forgiveness. His arms are available to shelter and protect the needed. His eyes are light and guide that leads to a good way. Get close to him to have a perfect company and to his presence will remain to safeguard your life.

131. THE WORLD

The world is so small that is why it is so complex. So large that the man cannot dominant, so small that day by day the man has less space. Many want to take over it, but they are as sand in the sea that even among themselves get confused. The world is a single family that is composed by fifteen members. Plants, animals, air, planets, seasons of the year, the Cardinal directions, cold, heat, water, Earth, light, darkness, humidity, odor and noise. The rest which are not listed, it is because they are derived from the same. For example, light, density, speed, scope and effect. The world couldn't resist if the Sun or the moon would be miss. Plants and animals would die from cold or heat. So on, each of them, are dependent on the other. The world is our family in which all we live. It isn't as cruel as is thought neither unfair as it is believed. It deserves our respect and care. It cries for honor and loyalty since it is very little receiving. Without it we can't live so it deserves our love and affection. The Creator handed it to us to enjoy it and not to destroy it. Give thanks to it for giving you drink, eating, breathe and where to lie down. Love this family that many ignore and others have it by enemy. They are killing it with chemical, with dynamites and poison to produce a lot and fast. Take Care and protect the world.

132. SOMEONE FOLLOWS YOU

I have always thought that I was or I will be alone to the empty, but behind my walk there is someone looking after me for not to fall to the abyss. Visible or invisible, he is there to save me of any danger. I have walked between the difficulties and to the empty infinite without thinking that someone was following me. I have lived in a low apathy without believing that others were suffering from my dark face. I was isolated without taking care of the crowd around me. I searched love when it was there in front of my face. I checked my path of life and I decided that one day I would have to change. To see the past to not commit the same mistakes. Remembering the past to improve what was fine. If possible, in the same place or with the same person. Be careful in all the steps and giving movements. Thinking about the result and the future consequences of acts and so do not look for a guilty. I always thought that I was or I'll be alone to the empty, but behind my walk there is someone looking after me for not fall to the abyss. Visible or invisible, he is there to save me of any danger.

133. THE MYSTERY

After a loss, there is a hope to replace the pain. After an error or failure, there is a purpose which expects to be won. Behind each problem, there is a reason to move on. Each obstacle, indicates that there are other options with better results. Barriers prove the ability to have and it is not weakness. Bass mood indicates that is due to think well in what is going to do and before continuing should be prepared to come. Strength can't master if there is no willing. Weakness hides the unspeakable and inaudible. You can reach all without anticipate the triumph.

134. TOGETHER FOREVER

No one impedes dreaming to be someone in this life. Because to whish something better, is natural and good. To lust, is bad. To envy, is harmful. You may have something today and tomorrow it will disappear. One day you feel on the top of the hill, next day you are in the swamp. What is life? I see many competencies to each other. Everyone runs at all time. All of them want to get to their destination. They obstruct each other on the way. Pass over the weak. They look the one who has something as well the other who is without anything. And what are the opportunities? They are those who come without notice. Knocking at the door to be received. Overlooking by the window to be seen. Making noise to be heard. Walking like cats for not bother to their lucky. They get tired of waiting and stand in the next door. If they are not well received and treated, will not come back even more than you pray, you cry, you will beg and humiliate before them. Life and the opportunity are a couple. A perfect marriage. It is an invisible being with hands and feet. It has eyes and ears. It has the five senses as any other human being. They walk, fly and travel from a place to another. Life and the opportunity, are one and no one can separate them.

135. THE LADY

I am an uncategorized woman. A humble lady with no ambition. Simple, who knows how to understand the weakness and strength. Able to understand others without prejudice. I am not a Queen or mean to be Princess. I am not of any high social level. My love has no conditions. My affection is priceless. My affection has no limit. I am a woman who value Likewise. I do not expect be given a flower or any gift. I first judge my own acts and after this others, if it is time to do it. I like to respect and show all my loyalty to whom treats me alike. I share my skills with those who want to receive them. I use my ability at all levels of life and in all social classes. I am social culturist no lack or abundance humiliates me. My unchanged principles and irreplaceable values make me breathe. In my vocabulary there are no obscene words. I am not beautiful, I only have beauty that no one can see. I am not pretty or beautiful, I only have sweetness as a source and nobody can enjoy if I do not give my permission. I do not sell love neither buy tenderness. I know how to love without requiring anyone with my feelings. I do not ask anyone to stay with me because sorrow compassion. I respect freedom and the own decisions and also the outside. Value me as I am and I do not ask any more from what I can be.

136. AN OFFERING

I give you a great acknowledgement,
I do not denied you my tender fidelity.
Beautiful woman who always smiles,
I ask you to trust me.
Receive a flower from my hands,
Which I give you with fervor.
Beautiful company and only Lady,
Do not be hopelessness in our bed.
My love and your love are in your hands,
Do not let them be treated as brothers.
Appreciated Princess without Palace,
There is too much space in my heart.
Walk around freely in Eden,
Before a danger pass in disdain.
I go between bunches of flowers,
Because they are my beautiful loves.
I have a great love to flowers,
Infinite love to roses.

137. LIFE'S PACT

This is me, a full man. A Knight category that there is not much in the world. A male in all the extension of the word that can be found only once in life. A person who knows to admit and accept what was right, and doesn't repeat what was wrong. He isn't used to swear or to promise something that is not in his hands. I say and I name things as they are. However, I have a default, when my similar ask me for help and support, I find hardly to say no, because I have my own principles that no one can misrepresent. I make my own decisions with conviction of the consequences against or in favor. I'm a being who knows how to respect the others and own. To keep loyalty as unique gift and honor and the Crown of effort. Morality directs me and guide my steps to happiness. Inside of me there is only Justice and equality as The Golden Rule. In my guts overflow good feelings. Constructed of love and in my veins live genuine love.

138. DESPERATE

When someone asks me, how much do you love me? My look responds, as a handle of ground. But my voice has no response because I don't know how to calculate. Whenever someone ask me, how far do you love me? My gesture argues, as up in hell. As a total reader, she replies me, does it exist? Shacking my head, unfortunately up there no, but here in this world yes. But I don't answer because I don't know how to divide neither to measure space. How far can you love me? A disguised smile as far as in the pantheon. A fulminant look, but why? With words under despair, because over there are no doubts, concerns or questions. When I'm in ecstasy, I hear a sublime voice, do you love me? That is when I get frozen dumb, blind without common sense and I wonder, where am I climbed? I only can think in three optional answers as a life-saving. One, I love you as to in hell where the fire of love burns without off for anything. Two, as up in the pantheon where it governs peace and tranquility. There is no noise, complaints, arguments or lawsuits. Three, as much as deep in the sea so you can drown me and then you revive me with your sweet kisses. Is this too much to ask? And I do not want to re-mainland non sorry, not to beg, be humbled and be slave of made-up love. I do not longer ask or looking for love because I'm tired of waiting. Everything is over.

139. THE BRIDGE

On one side of the River there is the man who cannot declare his love to the woman who loves. While in the other hand, is not usual to declare to a man. Both have saved the fire of love as dead steam in a pot. So long to wait and suffer for saying, my love. Here's the need for a reliable bridge to cross the river with its terrifying strength. It is also a postman without salary known as the best friend. The river, is the fear which drowns the feelings because not know how to express correctly feelings to a woman. Cowardice not to face the reality in front of a lady. To feel lower in front of an invaluable beauty. The fear of being rejected by anything. Non-die because the love they feel each other, the bridge and the postman are faithful servant. Cards flew without wrap without stamps. If these were not enough, the bridge assumed the role of editor. The content and authenticity of signature's sender, were in front the view of the bridge and the postman. The recipient never knew the letters or the words did not belong to whose was believed. However, she was confidential between her family, society and friends. There was all kind of suspicions suddenly the bridge found an invincible test invincible and fell, disappearing between the two lovers. By time and as they could, they built their own. They dominated the river's currents by swimming on them. Two years later, they formalized their relationship and joined their lives. They made the decision and finally reached the happiness. As a reward of their struggle and effort, they had kids of great satisfaction. It was a privilege and honored to serve two biggest loves.

140. SAFE BOX

In innocence, dignity is being protected.
In childhood, the privilege is saved.
The sublime power is in adolescence.
In youth, wisdom is shooting.
In the maturity, knowledge is acquired.
In the elderly, the experience is lived.
Inside four walls, the information is.
In the flowery field, practice is.
In every walk, the experiment is.
In the knowledge of making the good, the fault is.
In telling the truth freedom is.
The position of these qualities and features,
It's all a fortune in man's life.

141. THE DIFFERENCE

I came to this world to serve and not to be a nuisance. I grant the right to respect others and free to all. I step for others to succeed and not interject my rebel's interests. I am here to benefit others and not to injure my brother. I am not seeking wealthiest to die among thousands of angels. I try to have friends without money so they will remember me when I am not no longer with them. My hands are to lift the fallen and not to crush the weak. The bread that I hardly earn I share it with no hypocrisy. The knowledge that I have purchased, is to guide and enlighten those who do not have the same possibilities. Wisdom That I own, is not to condemn the ignorant but ignorance. The power that I have, is not for humiliate the weak but to praise him. I am willing to answer any nation requests. Suitable to meet what people cry out. Prepared to fill-up the mission that God has given to me. Trained to solve and not to complicate more than what is. I always look to mark the difference between the good and evil. Between the truth and falsehood.

142. THE CROSSING

I have traveled by roads and sidewalks since I am in the use of reason. I have crossed mountains and streams looking for your love. Winds blow furiously and succumb storm, turn off the light of hope for my misfortune. Risks and dangers in front of my walk, adverse which achieve the purpose of the destination. Looking for you day and night finally you appeared in the desert. I am not died because of thirst but because of sadness because your absence. I am not laying dying because of cold but because the lack of your heat. I am not hungry of love but of sweet kisses from your lips. I am not afraid of darkness but to not to have you with me. I am no run off font and springs but the sweet honey flowing your being. I have light but I do not have to you. What the money is good for, if you are not to me. What do I want for the mansion without your presence? In my awakening I see the Sunrises and get the moon, but you are not there. Being in Paradise without you, it is a step to cliff. A false movement, the fall to the abyss. The shape of myself, is you I follow your fingerprinting of happiness encourages you have layout in my path. The great reason not to fall.

143. A TRUE LOVE

I want to tell you today that I am very happy because there is a woman who loves me with all her heart, her soul and body. Knowing that I cannot offer her any comfortable and promising future. That I have nothing material I am totally on the street and still is willing to share her life with me. Threatening her safety and welfare facing all kinds of danger, critical and condemnatory judgment. She only thinks of happiness and love that matches us. This woman, is you, thank you for accepting me and greet me into your heart. Also, for letting me to be part of your feelings and to be participant of your love. You know that I only have for you, love, respect, good deal, loyalty, confidence and above all, unconditional love. I love you above any obstacle, barrier or adversities that could be interposed in our life. I want you to be next to me by the rest of my life. I have the dream and the desire of getting old next to you. My love, in the same way, I feel for you. You are a real man of God. A gentleman to me. A full man for me. A perfect love that I have looked for so long, I suffered to find you among the thorns of life.

Now, as we are intertwined. Let's cover each other with affection puree. Let's get lost in the infinite love and never come back to this cruel world which only makes cry and suffer without any cause. We live our true love.

144. LOOKING FOR THE GUILTY

Seems That I am guilty without having done any wrong against my parents. My mom, always speaks badly of my dad. She says that he is not worth to be called a father. That he is a farce, a hoax and destruction of my life. That he is not worth to love as such. To talk, to live together and to share the time, the time, it does not benefits me in anything. I wonder quietly, why did you procreate me with him? And not only me, but others. Did not you know what he was? Do you get together or marry him by forced? How I would like to be deaf in order to not listen to outside misfortunes because the same happens with my father. I wish I hadn't been born non to see and live the fault of strangers. My father says all kinds of curse of my mom. He prohibits me to go and see her and give her at least a hug. To give her a kiss as a child and tell her that I love her. It seems that both are offenders and enemies, having me in the middle of them without knowing which way to take. I also think that it is society is fault or maybe the same God is fault what I am witness, the attitude and the way my parents are. I do not have more strengths to keep being the Center of the balance. A single solution and only hope is that both tell me about the good thing that they lived and the best that they shared. I do not care if it was a long or short time. I do not care who was the guilty. I do not desire that they live together. I just want to live happy and in my memory save the best memories of my parents.

Printed in the United States
By Bookmasters